C000108166

Natasha Brook is a quirky, enigmatic and spontaneous woman, who just happens to be described more often than not as a wife, a mum, a daughter, a friend and an employee. Natasha holds down a full-time job and has built a career in the commercial world as a world class business developer. When she's not developing multi-million pound pan global deals she's quiet and rather a laid-back individual.

Having battled mental health all her life she's achieved some pretty amazing things. She's got two degrees, been on the UK's best loved Quiz Show, adopted a child and a dog and kept intact her marriage for over 20 years. Her friends think she's flamboyant, eccentric and a bit weird – but there's always fun to be had when Natasha is around.

To my family and friends, you are my world and I thank you for loving me.

Natasha Brook

THINGS WILL GET BETTER

*And then worse, then fine,
then really *f***ing terrible,
then good, then bad,
then better

AUSTIN MACAULEY PUBLISHERS™

LONDON • CAMBRIDGE • NEW YORK • SHARJAH

Copyright © Natasha Brook 2022

The right of Natasha Brook to be identified as author of this work has been asserted by the author in accordance with sections 77 and 78 of the Copyright, Designs and Patents Act 1988.

All rights reserved. No part of this publication may be reproduced, stored in a retrieval system, or transmitted in any form or by any means, electronic, mechanical, photocopying, recording, or otherwise, without the prior permission of the publishers.

Any person who commits any unauthorised act in relation to this publication may be liable to criminal prosecution and civil claims for damages.

All of the events in this memoir are true to the best of author's memory. The views expressed in this memoir are solely those of the author.

A CIP catalogue record for this title is available from the British Library.

ISBN 9781398420533 (Paperback)
ISBN 9781398420540 (ePub e-book)

www.austinmacauley.com

First Published 2022
Austin Macauley Publishers Ltd®
1 Canada Square
Canary Wharf
London
E14 5AA

Table of Contents

Introduction

Hey, I'm Nat. A massive thank you for picking up this book. I'm about to share with you some big moments from my life as I begin to process them for the first time. The reason the time is right to do this now is that I've finally been diagnosed with Emotional Unstable Personality Disorder (EUPD) and Attention Deficit Hyperactivity Disorder (ADHD). I'm learning what that means for me now in my adult life as at 46, I've hopefully still got a lot of life ahead! In sharing my story, I hope to help raise awareness of mental health and help others with similar mental health disorders. I also want you to laugh, giggle and chortle along the way – because life is serious enough and so we have to make sure we find the silliness and joy in things as we go.

I also want to share my life-long conclusion that people like me are the new 'normal'. Normal is a relative term, as who really can say what's normal or not? I refuse to accept that I am not some version of normal.

According to the World Health Organization (WHO), mental health is a state of well-being in which the individual realises his or her own abilities, can cope with the normal stresses of life, can work productively and

fruitfully, and is able to make a contribution to his or her community.

World Health Organization. Promoting mental health: concepts, emerging evidence, practice (Summary Report) Geneva: World Health Organization; 2004. [Google Scholar]

You Are Not Normal

I have been told on a number of occasions that I am not normal. I've been described as weird, quirky and eccentric. A couple of times exes have said that I'm mental or a psycho, which to be fair I probably was a little. I refer to myself as a bit mental and a bit weird – but, I do consider myself to be normal. I have a great job, a happy marriage going 23 years strong and am a mum. I adopted my daughter five years ago and have the most beautiful, zany, funny and clever 10-year-old girl. I reckon I must be able to get away with calling myself normal as I function in the 'normal' world quite well.

Going through the adoption process was when I really became aware that the 'world' at large didn't view me as normal. Nathan (hubby) and I had applied 4 years previous to start the adoption process and been turned down at the first meeting – apparently being overweight and having a BMI of 30 means you're not considered 'normal'. The fact I like cake and dislike exercise, I argued, made me exceptionally normal – but the social workers wouldn't have it. Their advice was to lose 7 stone and apply again. It took me 3 years to lose the 7 stone but I did it. I capped my calorie intake to 1200 calories a day and took up running. I got used to the food restrictions but I hated running. I tried spin class, yoga and badminton and a whole heap of other exercises but they weren't for me. I invested two grand in a gym grade running machine and four times a week I ran. Nowhere – but I ran.

Nathan and I applied again and this time we were told that the weight criteria had now been removed. In fact, it had been removed two and a half years previously, but no one in the council had thought it important to tell us! I'm not sure why it was removed and it was never explained to us, but apparently BMI was now considered not to be a reliable gauge of how 'normal' you are or how good of a parent you may be!

We were informed that the process would be in two stages. The first stage to see if we would be suitable candidates and the second stage to help us prepare and be supported to become parents. The first stage flew by but it was hard work. Our social worker asked us hundreds of questions and gave us lots of different parenting scenarios to consider and talk through. Nathan and I really applied ourselves and we enjoyed exploring the different views we held on parenting. Nathan's parents had been very liberal and intellectual parents who had applied their smarts to their parenting. Nathan's mum had been a stay-at-home mum – the sort of mum who had homemade cupcakes ready each night and was on hand to craft, do homework, and attend sports day and the class play. They'd lived in the same house all their lives.

My experience was entirely different. My dad was in the Army, and so my family and I were shipped around Europe quite regularly. We spent time in Germany, Austria and Ireland. That's three kindergartens and one primary school before we finally set up 'home' in K-town, West Yorkshire. My mum always worked hard manual labour type jobs, full-time minimum wage such as; school dinner lady, care worker or shop assistant and was a grafter. She'd come from a single parent family and been sent to work at age 13. My dad worked shifts in the army and when he left the army, he became a fireman. Firemen work two twelve-hour days followed by two twelve-hour evening/night shifts. This meant I rarely saw either of them at the same time. I had a lot of time with neighbours, child-minders and adults I hardly knew or liked. My parents came to school events when they could but this was not often. Maybe they came to one sports day over the course of my school life. I'm not going to lie, it did hurt when I got 'lead mouse' in the school play during primary school and neither parents could attend. Similarly, years later when I got cast as the 'in-keepers' wife for the nativity, there was no one in the audience for me that night either. I had resigned myself to not asking them to attend such events to avoid disappointment.

Discussing parenting styles and exploring how we might parent our child raised lots of unresolved issues for me. It also addressed a whole heap of questions I'd gathered over my life. Through the first stage of the process I realised I had abandonment issues – so learning about it and how to help an adopted child, I was able to work through the healing and therapeutic response. We were now ready to go to the final stage and be approved. We met the adoption panel and our case was presented to 15 unknown people deciding our future. The panel was made up of social workers, doctors, former adopted children and adoptive parents. During our session, we were asked to explain why we felt we'd make good adoptive parents. This was easy, an adoptee needs love, compassion, understanding and a chance to have their missing building blocks rebuilt. Nathan and I were prepared, honoured and ready to offer a home – filled with love and therapeutic parenting. We were told that we'd been approved but would now have to wait for the formal and final approval from the Lead Social Worker. Imagine our heartbreak when two weeks later our application was deferred.

Never in my life had I been so angry or upset. It felt as though our whole world had fallen apart. The approval that we were decent people, good humans, worthy and trusted to parent had been denied. Whilst coping with this outcome we also had to tell our dearest friends and our family that we had been deferred and explain why. For many of our friends and family, this would be the first time they learn I have a mental health disorder.

The road ahead was long and torturous but we found a social worker who believed in us. Well, someone who believed that a person with a mental health disorder could still be a good parent. She made a case on our behalf that examined our life through a social lens instead of the medical lens which is apparently what had stopped us. I had been diagnosed with Premenstrual Dysphoric Disorder in 2008. 2% of women suffer from this disorder. This presents ten days before my period and I get the onset of 'low mood'. It can also make you suffer with irritability, insomnia, anger outbursts, hypersomnia and anxiety. The adoptive appointed doctors had presented that my disorder would limit my ability to parent the child as a 'normal parent'. There's that word again – normal.

My social worker explained that if the doctors had presented that my disorder could prevent me from being a 'normal' person based purely on my diagnosis, we would have to demonstrate that I led a 'normal' life. We'd use a social model of normality to demonstrate I was 'normal'. The fact to be punctuated is that even though I don't feel 'normal' all the time (have an even mood), I still behave normally. Her comparison to what normal is was as follows:

1. I'd never been fired from a job.
2. I had been successively promoted year on year and was now a Director in a household named company.
3. I earned six figures a year.
4. I had been married for 21 years and we'd been together for 23.
5. Nathan and I still liked each other and had joint hobbies we enjoyed.
6. I was still in contact regularly with the parents and my brother.
7. I was still in contact with kids I'd been friends with at school.
8. I had a small network of close friends I could count on.

The social worker actually had to write and interview all my old bosses. That's ten companies and ten bosses. Our deferred application was finally approved. By the criteria set by the local council, I had finally passed their 'normality' test.

Once you pass you then have to find a child which is a hard process which was excruciating and much longer than you realise – but when you find your child, you know. We found Stella and she is everything we ever dreamed of. She was 5 when we first saw her on paper. Like every child born (whether they are adopted or not) they need love, stability, encouragement and safe and secure opportunities to develop.

We are coming up to Stella's tenth birthday and so Nathan and I take the time to reflect.

1. Are we doing OK?
2. Are we doing well enough?
3. Have we been therapeutic enough?
4. Will she have a normal life?

After our conversation, I reflected on my own childhood trauma and the ways that trauma can manifest and go completely undetected. I guess I had 4 significant experiences during my early childhood that created my complex trauma. I'm thankful for the adoption process as not only did it provide me with the opportunity to be a therapeutic parent to Stella, but it also enabled me to revisit my own experiences through a new therapeutic lens.

My trauma was endured in my very early life but was well hidden through the coping mechanisms I developed. To the naked eye, you wouldn't be able to tell. The fact I was popular at school, I had a best friend, my grades were good, I took part in school events – heck, I was even Head Girl in the 6th form. All these markers of telling if someone is normal or not would easily be ticked off any checklist. So let me tell you briefly about my trauma.

1. The first was simply attending many schools. This disturbed my ability to develop lasting friendships. Having to work quickly to make new friends, with kids who spoke different languages and had different

cultural norms from me. Never getting past the introduction and storming phases.

2. The second experience I recall was being trapped under a colossal fallen wardrobe while living in Minden, Germany. The wardrobe tipped over and its door swung open. As it fell the wardrobe swallowed me. It felt like being trapped in a mahogany coffin. I was too scared to call for help, and so I lay stuck for what seemed like hours. As I hadn't sustained any physical injuries the aftercare was a quick kiss and cuddle from my mum, with no real acknowledgment that I had been in their long time. The wardrobe was put back upright. The consequence of this was to develop hyper vigilance and to spend the rest of my life scanning my surroundings for risks, never able to relax. In tandem accepting that as I had been missing some time and no-one had actually missed me – that I was unimportant, insignificant to my caregivers.

3. The third experience involved our home being the target of a bomb attack while living in Ireland. Not many western kids can claim they've survived a bomb attack. The consequence of which led to us fleeing our home in the early hours and getting on a plane back to England, without any possessions.

4. The fourth and perhaps the most painful of all my early memories was being rejected by the local primary school when we finally returned to the UK. I was told that the 'school didn't want me'. In reality, the school was full, but the words 'the school doesn't want me' will haunt me for the rest of my days. Just more evidence that I was not worthy.

The sum of these experiences is Complex Childhood Trauma. We've had lots of time with Stella to help her address her own trauma and what has been super helpful is that I have been able to recognise behaviours quickly. The compliant child is one who isn't feeling secure and safe yet. The social butterfly child who hasn't been able to get past the point of making new friends and have enduring friendships. My own trauma experience has actually given me a better ability to identify these problematic behaviours and support Stella through them.

So in answer to our questions

1. Are we doing OK? Yes, we really are.
2. Are we doing well enough? Well, using the children's published milestones as a guide – she's meeting them all. She's getting great reports from school and is as able as her class peers. She understands her history and is comfortable telling her story to those she trusts. She is happy telling us what she needs and when she needs it. She can be a right pain in the arse (this is the biggest marker of success for me – she trusts us enough to know she'll still be loved even when she throws a strop!)
3. Have we been therapeutic enough? Only time will really tell us the answer to that but for now, we take comfort in the visible results. Stella can self-soothe, she can process emotions and does, she understands her life story and she can express herself.
4. Will she have a normal life? We have no idea.

Who decides what a normal life is anyway?

Challenging Normal

This book forms part of my own personal healing journey. There have been times when someone referring to me and my life as 'normal' would have been the highest compliment I might consider. Then there have been times when this label would enrage me. How dare someone think that the sum of my capability, adventurous spirit, intellect and capacity for love be 'normal'. I was insulted by this label. I am not normal – I am extraordinary. Of course, in reality both these viewpoints can co-exist.

There are times in my life I have been completely average and been glad to be so, and other times when I've appeared superhuman and surprised myself. This particular chapter of my life I think I bounced between these two states a lot. Admittedly I also dwell in the realms of weird – which is still OK.

Somebody posted a meme on Facebook that said:

'There is no normal, there are just slightly more popular versions of weird.'

This is where I have landed after a lifetime of consideration, research and self-discovery.

This memoire attempts to address what was one of the most difficult times in my life – the University Years. It's this experience where my childhood trauma revealed itself as my carefully crafted coping strategies became redundant. Every day felt like a new low or conversely euphoric high. I can't recall any amount of time longer than a day when by my own definition I could say I felt normal. It felt like a succession of days at war with myself. The general of this war had the advantage of knowing how to flank me, how to hit me hard, how to starve me of self-esteem, how to flood me with paranoia and when at my weakest take a hard-hitting, long affecting swipe. The problem with being at war in your own mind is that you can't find respite. You can't just ask for a truce, wave the white flag or send for reinforcements. However, what you can do is craft a range of battle responses, warring strategies and develop a set of impenetrable armour. Armour does weigh heavy though when you repeatedly wear it, day in and day out. So sometimes when you need to take it off and let your skin feel the air, the best way to do this is through the use of alcohol, and/or the use of drugs or other such distractions.

My distraction was sex. I could have easily titled this book 'How to pick up men in quick succession', as the truth is that was the way my trauma manifested itself and how my warring commander responded. It was not pretty. However, at its heart, the following story tells you of how a period of major transition and heartache sent me down a path of self-destruction. I will share in full gruesome detail the consequent coping tactics that some may find slightly weird, awkward, cringe-worthy, but damn right funny in places. It's also a story of a vulnerable young adult coping with undiagnosed mental ill health (it's OK – you are still allowed to laugh).

I managed to 'get through' 18 men in 18 months. Some people have said it should've been a wager – as at least there'd be some dignity in that. But no, this is my life, my truth, and I don't regret any of it. (Well, I do, in fact, regret some of it as some of it has brought back some terrible memories where I've blushed for days or felt nausea). But it's mine, nonetheless. Some of this is going to seem far-fetched, even made up for titillation or sensationalism – it is not, it's all real. I've changed the names to protect the innocent and partly as I can't remember all of them. I was prompted to write this memoir when I found 'the' piece of paper with the men's names inscribed upon it. I'd written them all down in 1996 and stuck it in the pages of my handwritten diary. I remember writing the list just in case I ever needed to go back to tell some of them that I now had contracted some rare STD, which they may now have – after a night of passion with yours truly. Even back then, I was wild but had a very serious and responsible side. I'm happy to report I've never had to use the list for breaking bad news of a deadly or incurable disease – because I was sensible. The fear of having to tell my parents I went to university on their working-class pound and all I got was an STD filled me with such dread I was always prepared – like a good girl brownie.

Each encounter is a unique story and might not be in order as when I wrote the list, I struggled to put them in sequence, but each meeting left an impression. Some deeper than others and some more vivid than others. Some get triggered by smell, sound, or taste. Like the extraordinary and unusual time I was having – they reappear in consciousness. Some like a long-lost friend and some – well, like a living nightmare. A couple makes me smile widely; one, in particular, makes me grin like an idiot. An idiot who had the best sex of her life. Mind-bending, toe-curling, multi-orgasming, fanny quivering, nipples tingling sex. I just had to pause for a second to let the wave of feeling pass over me. Some encounters make me giggle as I recall the fumbling and the damn right awkwardness of the situation. Finally, some make me grimace or wince with embarrassment. Only one left me with feelings of shame, which I'm still not quite ready to let go of yet.

In revisiting this time, I was able to finally process the emotions that I was unable to cope with at the time. I finally get to address the trauma but this time with more understanding and self-love. I share this recollection with you in the hope that some of you will recognise some of my behaviours in you. You may identify your reactions and thinking patterns as being similar. They might not be considered mainstream normal but amongst a growing population of men and women, you are 'normal'. By de-stigmatising poor mental health and recognising their needs to be a continuum of 'normality', we can find a place in the world, a tribe of like-minded people and many more can start their own healing journey with acceptance and understanding.

The first story was the catalyst, the reason I began to self-detonate. It's the story of my first love, and the significant transition from home to university and the consequences on my mental health. At times this is a hilarious combination and at other times it's devastating.

I'm Just a Shy Girl

It all started in 1992. I'm a massive fan of The Smiths and The Cure. Yes, I'm an 'alternative' young woman. I'd begun to blossom into this weird and wonderful individual from the age of 16. I had the nose ring, the dyed red hair and sported a lot of black clothing. I told people I was a Goth (but I was still secretly listening to Rick Astley). However, I was ready to be taken seriously as an adult. It was the year I was taking my final year of A' Levels. Business Studies, Economics, German and General Studies. I actually wanted to be a graphic Designer. My mum and dad had other plans for my career – I would be an international business leader and so as not to disappoint; I dropped all pursuits of artistry and followed their instruction.

Although I'm taking subjects I don't really enjoy, it's actually one of the best times of my life. It was 6th form all week, followed by work on a Saturday. I worked at the local Retail Pharmacy in my small northern town. It paid well, and the Saturday crew had a good laugh. In fact, I met my life-long best friend Sarah there. I'd always had a best friend at school – Annie, but we were very different. She was timid and low maintenance. She didn't need the limelight and was happy to hold my coat and bag at school while I hogged it.

She wasn't allowed out on the weekends albeit she did have a Saturday job at a local shoe shop. She too was a card-carrying virgin. Annie was a really sweet girl. When we were younger she used to share her chocolate biscuit with me during lunch breaks. Her mum would make her a different sandwich each day and pack a packet of Cadbury's squares. I actually think Annie asked her mum to only pack these so she could share them with me. She also had a yoghurt and a packet of crisps in her lunch box. My lunch box was the same every day. Salmon paste sandwiches. I never got crisps, yoghurts or chocolate in any form. I think Annie felt a bit sorry for me and so would always go out of her way to share with me. This even extended to taking German at A-Level because she knew how important it was to me and didn't want me to be the only student taking it. She was petite, with a really pretty face and striking white blonde curly hair. Wherever we went, teachers and adults would comment on how striking her blonde hair was. I was pretty envious of that hair I can now admit! Annie was not like me in any way. I was – no, am loud, appear over-confident and am socially awkward. The latter is code for inappropriate. I'm inappropriate, but I don't mean to be. The life lessons smaller children learn about how to make friends, how to behave as normal functioning children were missed. I missed all the socialising lessons, apparently!

My home was always filled with raised voices, I can't remember a conversation where 'inside voices' would be used. In part because as it turns out my mother has severe hearing loss, and also in part as my parents never seemed to be in the same room. Our first home in the UK was an ex-council house. You entered through the side door into a tiny kitchen, which had a door that led into the only other downstairs room. This was the living room. It seemed large to me but it only held basic furniture. A sofa that sat three people and a fireplace. We had a colour TV and all of us would squeeze onto that sofa. As my brother Alan got older, he would hang with his friends in the evening, so there seemed to be more room for the three of us. Alan is four years older than me. He has always been an 'outdoors' type of person and so as soon as he was allowed to go outside with his 'mates', he was gone. He was always in trouble and from a very early age behaved as though he had the freedom and capability of a mature teen. Consequently, he'd go missing a lot as he wouldn't think twice about meeting an older boy, befriending him and going on untold adventures. So when he did eventually reappear at home both parents would be yelling at him. Over the course of our childhood, it became the expectation that he would go missing and when he'd return, arguments and punishments would be bestowed. Alan just did not care. There wasn't a punishment they hadn't tried and none of these remedies ever curtailed his actions or ambitions in being a lone ranger. One particular day he had gone out in the morning and met up with a much older boy whose family of travellers were situated on the local field. They'd played with each other all day, even sharing a meal at lunchtime, but then they'd disagreed about something and the older boy had punched Alan. Trust me, spending more than 30 minutes with Alan makes most people want to punch him. He's got arrogance and attitude in equal measure. I liken it to small dog syndrome. The smaller the dog the noisier and aggressive they tend to be. They front up to bigger dogs and have confidence way beyond their size. This was Alan. Alan was unable to accept the punch as a signal to retreat and leave and so decided to engage in a brawl. He'd have been 11 and his competitor about 15. Alan had got in a few scrappy punches and twirled the young boy around by his leather blouson jacket. In doing so, he'd torn the jacket. After the altercation, the boy had yelled, "I'll get my dad, and he's gonna kill your dad – you'll see!"

Alan then ran home and told my mum and dad about what had happened. Alan was also a bull-shitter. Even from a young age. So we heard about a whole gang of youths who had descended upon him and he'd valiantly fought them off. As he retold his version of the fight his heroics were trebled in size. My mum and dad listened but had genuine worry on their faces. The field where the travellers were living was 200m away from our house. Within minutes we had a marauding gang outside our house. My mum grabbed me and Alan and we ran to crouch under the living room bay window. The boy's father was yelling in Gaelic at our house. My dad had gone outside to discuss the matter with the boys family. I seemed to be crouched under that window for a long time and I could hear voices but I couldn't make out what was being said. I remember being so very frightened. My dad is a strong bloke, but he's only 5' 8. He doesn't have any features that would make him appear menacing and I was sure he was just about to take a beating. We then heard the skirmish. A punch making contact with flesh. I started to cry, and so did my mum. I was trembling and remember being so scared I could hardly breathe. My brother kept popping up to look out the window which was really increasing my anxiety levels. As soon as he heard the punch he popped up to have a look. I'm not sure what happened because I'd zoned out of the present but the next thing I remember was my mum yelling for me and Alan to stay where we were and she ran towards the kitchen. As it turned out the boy's dad had heard of how he had punched Alan first. That his boy who was, in fact, 16, had punched Alan so hard it had lifted him off his feet. In the traveller community, it was apparently frowned upon for a young man to start a bare-knuckle fight with anyone younger than he. So the punch we had heard was the boy's father punching him. To demonstrate the point, that you don't pick on people that you are bigger/older than you, and to teach him a lesson. My dad had spoken with the boy's father to explain that Alan was a scamp and had a temper and that he would pay for the tear to his jacket, but he had expected that they address their boy as a 16-year-old picking on an 11-year-old was out of order. This had led to the traveller addressing his boy 'in their ways'. My dad had tried to intervene to explain it wasn't necessary but clearly the boy's dad thought it was. This is just one of the hundreds of examples of the scrapes Alan got himself into. He lived for them. He needed attention all of the time, and negative attention was what he'd practised the most. So between the yelling, raised voices and generally being a 24/7 spectator event, I watched Alan's life choices get worse and worse. I crafted a way to become invisible. If I was invisible, then I wouldn't get yelled at. If I was always sensible and good, then I wouldn't get smacked. The problem with this plan was that the less hassle I was, the more I was used as a weapon by my parents.

Why can't you be more like Natasha?
Why can't you get good grades like Natasha?
Why can't you get a school report like Natasha's?

Inevitably resentment grew, it festered and it spilt over in Alan's temper. There were times he was so angry with this comparison that he'd lock me in our bathroom for hours on end. A couple of times I told my parents which ended up with him getting told off or even smacked. This would come back full circle to me and he'd beat me up as soon as we were left alone. So then I had to become even more invisible. Be no problem for my parents and not appear successful or else face a beating from my brother.

At school, I'd always been the tallest girl and heaviest. Yep. I'm a chubster. I'm 5' 8 tall, brown bobbed hair, a UK size 16 and I'm pretty average to look at. I'm not ugly or unattractive or anything but I'm averagely pretty. My quick wit and barbed sense of humour were what attracted people to me. I'd had boys fancy me but none that I'd fancy back. It had got to the point where pretty much every 6th former had a notch on their bedpost but me. Not even close. I was so confident with my girlfriends and class peers but the polar opposite with boys. I was funny, chatty and sociable but put me within a metre of a boy I fancied, and I had zero conversation. No skills. Nada. Even the fugly (f*ck Ugly) kids had done it. Those with zero personality, poor hygiene, and no GCSEs. Imagine my shame! I had secretly pined away from the age of 15 for a boy at school called Chrispin. I can guess what you are thinking – what an awful name. But the posher the boy's name, the more I'd probably fancy them. He'd transferred into the school midterm. His parents were mega-rich, and his dad had taken over the local catalogue empire. I've always been attracted to 'posh', and he was. He was a tall boy and was quite chunky. I felt sure no one else would fancy him, and somehow he'd guess I liked him, and just like in the movies, he'd make some romantic gesture to show me that he'd been harbouring a crush too. John Hughes has a lot to answer for – as it turns out life is not like 'Pretty in Pink'. It all came crashing down when during work experience week – the school 'bike', Lisa got off with him. The school buzzed with the gossip.

How could this have happened? I knew Lisa. She didn't go for boys like Chrispin and preferred mainstream boys. She'd been through a lot of them already! I was heartbroken and crestfallen. I'd had 12 months to make a move and never had. Why was I so painfully shy that it'd meant I'd missed my chance? He'd only ever be her cast off at best now.

It was nearing Christmas, and our mutual friends Anya and Cady were having a house party. There were rumours that some of last year's 6th formers would be in attendance. So with my best jeans and going out top on, hair coiffed to within an inch of its life – I attended with high hopes. Annie and I made our usual wallflower impression and retreated to the bathroom.

"Well, this sucks," I said.
"It's alright," she said pitifully.

To be fair, she's never allowed out, so this was probably the most excitement she'd had all year. We had a bottle of orange Mad Dog 20/20 – the teenage drink of choice. We also had a 2-litre bottle of cider for show. Neither of us were drinkers, and we were struggling to neck the Mad Dog. My heart just wasn't in it. As we'd climbed the stairs, Lisa had seen us and waved. She was sitting on Crispin's knee in the living room, looking all loved up. The day's gossip had been rife with how they'd finally 'done it.'

"Can't believe they've finally done it," I said viciously.

"He's probably got an STD now as Lisa's been 'round the bike shed a few dozen times," Annie said rather matter-of-factly. We both giggled. In truth, Lisa was a sweet girl who had received the gift of a small frame and huge breasts. This was the recipe for lots of boy attention.

"She's a real skank," I continued. "And what's her hair doing?" I gesticulated wildly about my head.

She was growing out a very short hairstyle and to manage the mop she'd taken to drowning her head in wet look gel.

"I know she looks like a reyt skank," Annie slurred in proper Yorkshire dialect.

OK, maybe the Mad Dog had now started to work. There was a knock on the bathroom door.

"Guys, it's Lisa – I really need a pee. Let me in."

Annie and I shot each other a look. Shit! Had she heard us, we wondered. Reluctantly, I opened the door and smiled weakly.

"Hi Lisa," I said.

"Hi Nat," she said.

This really irritated me. Only my family and BFF were allowed to call me Nat. To you, skank, it's NATASHA!

"Great party!" she said. "Suppose you've heard about Chris and me?" She asked.

We smiled and responded with an obligatory 'Ummm, no, what?'

"We did it," she said. "Last night." She was smirking and behaving like a pompous cow.

"Oh, oh, right," Annie responded.

She knew I was probably choking back tears of rage. She knew me very well.

"It was so romantic. We were at Chrispin's house, which is massive. His mum and dad are on a business trip, so we knew we wouldn't get disturbed. I was only going to let him finger me, but you know…it just happened. We are so in love."

She was hovering over the toilet, and we could hear the pee hitting the toilet water.

"Well, if you're in love," I responded sarcastically.

"We really are." She smiled. "I didn't ever think of Chris in that way, it's been a bit of a surprise to us both. You know me – I prefer fitter boys, but he's just so sweet."

Annie and I just listened with silly smiles on our faces.

"Well, enjoy the party," she said and left.

I had never felt such rage as I did at that moment. Lisa hadn't even fancied him! She only thought he was sweet. I, on the other hand, had gone to sleep every night for a year rehearsing the moments we'd spend together. The moment I'd finally ask him out. Our first date, kiss and every little detail in-between. I'd spent most of my GCSE year staring at him. Besotted. The audacity that she'd basically gotten off with him, for something to pass the time during work experience was too much to bear. The rage burst through my veins, and I sprang up from the floor, grabbed the 2-litre bottle of cider, and unscrewed the cap frantically. I ran to the top of the stairs. Lisa was making her way back down the stairs. I tipped the bottle upside down and, with utter vitriol began to spill the cheap cider over her. I didn't plan it. I also didn't realise just how heavy a 2-litre bottle of cider was, and as it swilled up and down, I lost my grip. Essentially, I launched a nearly full bottle of cider towards her. At that very second, she stopped to look up the stairwell to find out why she was getting wet. The bottle hit her. It hit her hard. It hit her hard in the face. I took a sharp gasp in. Holy FUUUUUUUCK!!!

Just at that exact moment one of the older boys appeared and screamed, "The Police are here – RUN!" Panic and chaos ensued. People appeared from everywhere. Bedroom doors springing open and people buttoning up blouses and zipping up trousers. To this day, Lisa never knew what or who hit her. Sorry, Lisa. Well, kind of sorry. Perhaps I'm more apologetic for starting the rumour that she let Chrispin stick a cider bottle up her – which owned her the nickname of cider bottle Sue. It haunted her. She told me one day that she didn't know how people could be so mean. I had consoled her and told her not to worry, her real friends knew it wasn't right and other platitudes of bullshit.

Throughout this book, I'm going to give you a lot of stories where you won't like me. That's OK. I don't like me much in some of the stories, either.

The Grinning Rat

Sarah (my new bestie) and I met one Saturday morning on shift. I'd gotten a Saturday job working in my local retail pharmacy shop. Sarah is so lovely and chatty, and we got put on the hair aisle of the shop floor. She started chatting to me, and all I remember is that we never stopped laughing. My shift seemed to be over in record time, and we had become inseparable. We were both overjoyed to learn that we lived in the same village outside of K-town. This meant we could carry on chatting on the bus ride home. It was as if we had been best friends for life. Sarah was very worldly compared to me. Well, OK – not sophisticated, but she'd had a lot of boyfriends, and she'd had sex. So I felt a little in awe of her. She could teach me how to meet boys, I thought.

K-town, where I now lived and had lived for 10 years, was 'home'. It was and still is a working-class northern town, made famous by its tragic burning factory in the 1920s which gave rise to the common day 'Factories Act'. Most people who live there grew up to either work in the main factory, or if you'd 'done well' at your A' Levels, you'd work at the Bradford and Bingley building society headquarters. Not me. I was going to get out of there, I don't know why I was so driven to do so, but I knew it wasn't for me. Maybe it was because I couldn't see the attraction of living in a small town. We had a bus station, a post office, a Woolworths and an indoor market – but that was about it. The most exciting shop that ever came to K-town was The Body Shop. It was akin to Leeds getting Harvey Nichols. To secure my exit from this town I'd applied to Bournemouth Uni, Cambridge (Poly) and Leeds Uni and had received conditional offers.

I had applied to read International Business (with German). I would get a job in Germany, where I'd meet my prince charming. He'd be tall, fair-haired, blue-eyed and an intellectual. Maybe a professor or something exotic like a Nuclear Physicist. We'd meet at work and fall in love. We'd buy a Huff haus and have the obligatory 2.5 children, and he'd probably win a Nobel Prize for something brilliant. I had very, very high expectations for this poor bloke. He basically represented the polar opposite of the crappy life I'd had in this small crappy town. Imagine the shock of then meeting the 'one' in this small shitty town.

It was an ordinary Saturday night. Sarah and I went back to her house after work (she still lived with her folks) to get ready for our weekly pilgrimage to 'The Grinning Rat' pub in K-town. Sarah's house was an old Victorian terrace with four floors. Her mum and dad both worked and when we arrived they would be lying on sofas watching Gladiators on TV. They did have a spell in Saudi Arabia and so I kind of think this is why I have an infinity with Sarah. She gets the living abroad thing. Just like me, she's also way too quick to share personal details and stories. Her openness and lack of personal boundaries are a mirror for my own behaviour and I guess this makes me feel normal. She's also slightly plump and this means we can share clothes. Her home is in dire need of walls and decoration which again is similar to what I've become used to. My parents bought houses that needed structural makeovers and so I was used to not having bathrooms or electricity in each of the houses the flipped. Sarah had done the best she could with her bedroom. She had open brickwork and it was freezing in her room but she had posters on her walls and multiples of blankets and throws on her bed. Her dressing table was filled with pots of gel and bottles of mousse as Sarah had thick brown curly hair. It was untameable at the best of times but the beautiful round curls really suited her face. She had a really round face with massive blue eyes. She'd be smiling whenever I'd catch her gaze. She was a natural glass half full girl which was a great compliment to my glass being permanently empty. Her voice was always a bit louder than it ought to have been for any room we were in, but she didn't care. Sarah is a few years older than me and originally from London. She still speaks like a Londoner too. Her parents moved her in her last year of school, which led to her exam results not being great. She was now doing a secretarial course at the local college alongside working on a Saturday with me. Her goal in life was to get married and have kids. We were total opposites. She had befriended me in a way that was what I needed. She loved me deeply. She cared for me deeply. I'd never had a friend who was so devoted to me before and me to her. Twenty plus years later, I still feel the same way about her.

It's a fair old bus ride into K-town, so by the time we got back from our Saturday shift – we had to get ready quickly. Thankfully in those days, we didn't have to contour our faces, and in fact, we had a tiny makeup bag. Sarah and I both suffered from acne, so it mainly consisted of squishing zits and then moaning that our concealer wasn't strong enough to cover them up. We shared lipstick as neither of us used handbags, so everything we had fit into jeans pockets. On the bus into town, we'd get hyped. As we passed through each village we'd pull up at the bus stops and check out the people getting on the bus. The villages were traditionally filled with slightly older families. We'd talk about who we hoped would be in the pub once we got into town. For me, it was simple – Luke. Luke was tall, lanky, and blonde with blue eyes. He was a poshie and was training to be an architect. We'd been talking to each other for several months every Saturday night. He never made my list of conquests. He was indeed the one that got away. I'll tell you all about it later in the book, and it's heart-breaking – so spoiler alert – read that chapter with a box of tissues nearby.

Anyway, Sarah, on this particular night, was lamenting over Gianni, who was a tiny little bloke who worked in an engineering firm as an apprentice. He was dark-haired and swarthy (apparently) with Italian heritage. Sarah thought he was the sexiest of all combinations. However, in my eyes, he was a really short bloke with average looks. She'd been chatting him up over several weeks and gotten nowhere. He liked the attention but wasn't planning any time soon to put her out of her misery. The Grinning Rat pub was the destination for any self-respecting alternative 6th former or young adult. It was the holy grail of destinations due to the music it played. The Juke Box was primed with alternative music, including The Stone Roses, Pink Floyd, Metallica, Guns and Roses, Radiohead, Nirvana, Oasis and Blur. These were the staples of any alternative 90s teen. It didn't really matter what the jukebox contained though as Andrew (an acne-ridden boy from my school) would go there straight from his shift at Morrisons and basically spend his entire wage on playing The Stone Roses on repeat. We'd get there at 8.30, and they'd turf us out at 11 pm. Thanks to Andrew, we were subjected to the same songs on rotation.

Once the pub closed, we got shunted into the adjoining building, which was called 'The Rat Trap' and was the local nightclub. This was filled with an older crowd, and it played chart music. No one from The Grinning Rate was ready to go home at 11 – so you had to just grin and bear it. Sarah loved chart music, so the first half of the night was a drag for her, and I hated (publicly but secretly loved) chart music. We each took one for the team.

The Night I Fell in Love

So back to the main event. Sarah and I were in the corridor between the pub and the club. It was a really great place to hang out. You could see everyone coming and going. A place to look casual but secretly stalk your prey. It was also where the toilets were, so virtually everyone at some point had to come past us. I was whinging as Luke hadn't come out.

"Why would you not come out?" I asked. "It's Saturday night for god's sake!"

On the odd occasion I didn't see him, I used to take it very personally. I'd spend all week looking forward to our casual encounter – followed by utter nonsense and bollocks of conversation. It really didn't matter what we discussed. Most of the time, it was me filling the gaps, and Luke just looking relieved. His friends would squawk around us, but over time we had all got to know each other, and they were respectful of my valiant efforts to get off with their shy friend.

"Don't worry about it," Sarah had said.

This really pissed me off. Sarah meant stop whining – I don't care as Gianni's here. Now, if it was the other way around, she'd be nursing her wounded heart, and I like to think I'd be a bit more caring. In truth, if Luke was out, I probably would have encouraged her to get off with anyone, so I could concentrate on making Luke laugh. I had found that that was my secret weapon – laughter. Remember, I said I was inappropriate? Well, it turns out in the right conditions (in a club with alcohol), I'm quite funny. I used to make Luke laugh, and I enjoyed it. So the thought of him not being there was going to be a real buzz kill. We eventually migrated upstairs, where the real trendy crowd hung out. There was a little nook where you could stand and see the whole of the upstairs and downstairs. I made a beeline to it. It was also a beautiful place to be invisible. When I turned the corner to enter the nook, '*he*' was there. A tall, handsome man. He was probably 6' 2 in height, shoulder-length wavy mousy brown hair, and his face – well, he was beautiful. He had big full lips, almond-shaped eyes, and a perfectly proportioned nose. He was almost porcelain white with a flush of pink colouring in his cheeks. He was swigging ale from a Newcastle brown ale bottle. I realised that I hadn't taken a breath, I'd literally stopped breathing. I took a gasp, which must have been a strange noise as he turned to face me and asked,

"You alright?"

His eyes were full and twinkling. His lips were fuller than I thought, and there was a hint of a slight lisp.

"Err, yes, I think so. Sorry, I didn't realise anyone was 'round here." I motioned to the nook.

"Yes, I'm hiding from my brother. He's a tosser, and I don't want to see him." He smiled.

Oh, crikey, what a smile. My nether region had an immediate reaction, an immediate quiver.

"Oh right, I have one of those. Brothers that is. Who are tossers." We both smiled.

"The music in this place is so bad," I continued. I had noticed that he was wearing a Nirvana tee shirt.

"Yes – it's wank," he responded.

Well, the conversation didn't get any more exciting or intelligent, but it did go on until 2 pm and chucking out time. I had managed to find the conversation and use actual words, and he'd responded! This had never happened before. My stomach was in knots, and I don't think I drank any of my drink. I'd found myself watching him. The way his lip curled up to the right when he spoke. The way he kept gently pushing his curls over his perfect ear, and it relentlessly kept coming untucked. His hair was so silky soft it glistened. He kept making himself laugh, and I like the way he laughed from his lower abdomen. I'd noticed so much about him by the time the lights were turned on for kicking out time.

Sarah found me outside where I was standing with him.

"Who is this?" she asked, giving me a wink.

"Oh, err I don't actually know?" I giggled. "We didn't do names yet."

"Sam," he proudly announced.

I smiled widely. *Yes, that will do nicely,* I thought.

"Natasha," I added.

"Sarah, if either of you cares?" she said giggling.

I rolled my eyes. She's a joker is our Sarah.

Sarah motioned to me and asked, "Are we gonna get a taxi now?"

I couldn't think of any reason why I'd be able to say no, so I smiled weakly.

"Yes, suppose so."

The three of us walked to the nearest taxi rank, and Sarah went in and ordered the taxi.

They said it'll be a few minutes.

Why? Why? Every bloody week we went to the same taxi rank and had to queue to order a taxi and wait at least 20 minutes. So why tonight would we be serviced in a few minutes! Not fair. Seeing my reaction, Sarah motioned to me.

"Hey Nat, you clearly don't want to go home yet so look I'll give you my last tenner and just come back when you're ready. I'll leave the door open for you."

That was so Sarah. She'd give me the shirt off her back if she thought it would help me out. Sam overhearing us chirped in, "Hey, look, I work so I can pay for a taxi – if you want to hang out a bit longer?"

Oh my god. It was happening. I had found someone who I didn't repulse. Someone who wanted to hang out with me! So of course, acting cool I just said,

"If you're sure?"

Sarah grabbed my arm showing real concern and whispered to me, "I'm not sure, Nat."

"Look," he said. He reached into his combat pants pocket and took out his wallet. He opened it up and gave me a ten pound note.

"There, Sarah, she's got the cash and can go home anytime she wants," he added. Sarah smiled.

"OK, then, but if Nat is not back by 4, I'm calling the police."

We both smiled and waved Sarah off into her taxi and then turned to each other.

"Right, where do you want to go?" I asked.

In reality, there was nowhere to go. Back in those days after 2 pm everything other than the kebab shops and pizza places was closed. I couldn't face eating in front of him. I

41

knew it was serious as having a dirty kebab after the club was tradition. In actual fact, I loved that part of the evening. The chilli sauce dripping between your fingers and generally onto your jeans to leave a mysterious stain. Not tonight. This night needed to be free from my gluttonous chops devouring kebab meat and dropping salad down myself.

Sam held out his hand, and I took it. We started to walk. It was eerily quiet and I swear you could hear my heart which was beating loudly and erratically, as I kept forgetting to breathe. After a few short minutes, we were in the town hall square. It's a charming square. There are benches all around its perimeter, and a war memorial in the middle which kind of gives you a little privacy from the main road.

"Shall we sit here?" Sam asked.

"Yes, sure," I said coyly.

We sat down, and he put his arm around my shoulders. *Wow,* I thought. We chatted for some time when out of the periphery of my eyes, I saw a figure coming towards us.

"Oi Oi Oi, Nats!" came from a loud and booming male voice.

"Wait till I tell your dad you're canoodling in the square," and with that a loud bellowing laugh.

As they got closer, I realised it was my cousin Rob. I didn't know him well. We saw each other at family dos, but he was considerably older than me and we'd never really talked before. I smiled at him.

"Fill your boots then," he chortled as he walked past.

"You're a local celebrity!" Sam commented.

Perfect! I look popular. I won't tell Sam who it is and I'll just take the cool points, I thought. It was now approaching 4 am, and so I motioned to Sam that we needed to make a move.

I also now had a freezing cold body and numb bum from sitting on the park bench. I'd have happily stayed there all night, but a promise to Sarah was a promise. I started to move, and Sam pulled on my arm, and somehow, I magically fell back into him and just like a really cheesy rom-com he leaned in to kiss me. Now, full disclosure, I'm a bit of a kissing expert (in my own mind). The kiss is everything to me. It has to have 6 essential components:

1. The proper technique (not too hard and not too soft).
2. Lips which are full and moist – can't be kissing dry or chapped lips.
3. Fresh breath (not stale ale or cigarettes).
4. A small amount of tantalising tongue (not search party tongue).
5. Pressure counts for a lot. Too little and I get the mental heebie-jeebies, too much and my neck cricks.
6. A build-up – slow to start but building pace and intensity.

This one boy at school had kissed me, and it was like kissing two slimy cold slugs. He really liked me and kept trying to get off with me during school dances and parties and I kind of felt bad for him so every now and then I'd kiss him. But it made me feel a little sick. His lips were limp, flaccid and weak. I made a promise to myself that I'd never compromise on the kiss ever again after this.

This was the moment of truth. Sam's lips touched mine. Not too hard and not too soft. Moving in a smooth rhythm, building tension. I felt a huge rush. Tingling began to appear in parts of my body that I'd not felt before. The pace building and tension rising. It was literally perfect. As blood began to circulate to parts of my body, I started to worry. *What if he's expecting more?* As a card-carrying virgin, I wasn't ready to be deflowered on a park bench in the town centre. I'd always imagined a centrally heated bedroom somewhere with flattering lighting! I pulled away and quickly stood up.

"I really do need to get a taxi," I said, smiling. He made sure I got into a taxi after we exchanged landline numbers.

When I arrived at Sarah's, she was awake and waiting for me to tell all.

"There's not much to say," I said grinning like a Cheshire cat.

It was the sort of smile where your face would ache in a minute as your muscles in your face just couldn't support that wide of a smile.

"Yeah, yeah," Sarah said in a mocking tone. "Did you kiss?"

I genuinely couldn't speak. If I tried, I knew it was going to just be a squeak.

"Was it good?" Again, I just smiled like a lunatic.

"OK, well, get into bed and get some sleep – I want details tomorrow!"

But Did You Do It?

Sam and I saw each other a lot. We feasted on each other's musical knowledge, and we found lots to talk about, and we had lots in common. He was very well researched and took delight in telling me all about the many bands 'I had to listen to'. I was happy to be schooled. There was lots of kissing and some over the shirt action over the following weeks. Then one night while walking back towards the taxi rank, Sam noticed that the gate to a tiny shopping arcade was open. This essentially was an old Victorian passageway. He pulled me into it and started kissing me – heavy and hard. *Woah – Woah – Woah, tiger, I'm not ready for where I think this is heading.* Strangely my body disagreed. I was very aroused, and my head was buzzing and fuzzy. I could feel the moistness between my legs and throbbing had started. Hands were moving all around and over me. Touching, squeezing and generally going into clothing. This was new territory for me. Then I felt his hand go down the front of my jeans. *Abort! Abort!* my mind screamed. I reacted by pushing him away.

"I'm not ready for this," I stuttered looking towards the ground, not daring to meet his gaze. "Well, not here anyway."

"Oh, OK. Well, where?" he asked. I noted his tone was calm, and he didn't seem mad.

"It's just I've not done this before," I said, not breaking eye contact with the ground.

I knew I'd have this conversation one day, but it still got stuck in my throat. He'd think I was such a loser or worse undesirable. That no other man had ever found me attractive enough to have sex with me so I must be unattractive.

"OK, so let's take our time and when we get a suitable place and opportunity, and you're ready, we can try again." He smiled and pulled me towards him with his hand cupped behind my head. I instinctively nuzzled into his chest, I felt safe, respected and relieved.

Well, the perfect opportunity was about to present itself. My friend Page was having a house party, and we were invited. She lived in a sprawling Victorian house with several floors. We'd arrived early to preview our room options. Sam and I passed knowing glances towards each other. We knew that by the end of this party, we would have taken our relationship to the next level. We socialised with everyone, and throughout the evening, couples disappeared. We'd been drinking cider and talking about music as usual. We'd talked about going to Glastonbury together, and tickets were being released that weekend.

"I'll buy them, and you just pay me back when you can."

"Of course. I'm getting a full-time job over summer before uni so can pay you back pretty quickly," I responded.

We continued to discuss the line-up: Robert Plant, The Black Crowes, Belly, Red Hot chilli Peppers, Henry Rollins, and so many other acts. Sam then took my hand. I knew that the portion of the evening I'd been secretly dreading but secretly ridiculously excited for was upon us. I'd been casually chatting nonsense all evening, but my mind had been firmly fixed on this moment. I was ready or else I was as prepared as I was ever going to be.

We found a room up in the attic space. No bed. But an array of floor cushions. Most importantly, no lamps. I didn't want any light creating ambience or highlighting my bulky silhouette. I was nervous. Not about the sex – but about him seeing my rounded stomach. It's fair to say I'm body-conscious. I'd been taunted all my life for being a fat girl, bigger boned and tall. There hadn't been lots of name-calling or teasing as I'd managed to get myself a firm place in the girl's popular hierarchy and so this warded off most nasty comments. However, every name I had been called in my life had stuck. From a very early age, I knew I was bigger than most girls. I was the tallest girl in the school from the age of 7 until I was 15. Thankfully at 15, a transfer pupil joined our school, and she was taller! However, she was slim, and so this made my frame look heavy. I knew I had a belly. I'm not talking about a gentle curve; I'm talking about a full-on apron style stomach. I just couldn't comprehend how I would disguise it. No amount of posture was going to hide it. Well, it was too late now. Things were happening. As we kissed, I was aware that Sam had now climbed on top of me. It all happened so quickly. One second, we were kissing and the next he was getting off me. Had I missed the main event? I wasn't sure what had happened or what was happening, but Sam was zipping his trousers up and jumping to his feet.

"What's up…what's happening?"

"It's me, I'm a loser!"

With that, he turned and disappeared through the door. My head was spinning. What was happening? What had I done? I was trembling. I reassembled my clothing quickly. I wanted to run after him to see what was going on, to undo anything I'd done that had upset him. I worked my way downstairs and got to the kitchen. People were still in their chatting. My friend Steven looked up and saw me.

"If you're looking for Sam, he just left," he said motioning to the door.

I exited into the dark night where the road was pitch black. There were no street lights. I couldn't really see anything or anyone. I then felt something in my stomach. It was a painful feeling. It was intense. I can only describe it as the feeling of severe panic, anxiety, loss, and nausea. It was so fierce I doubled over. I realised I hadn't been able to breathe for a few moments. What was this feeling? I couldn't shake it. I felt like I wanted to run and never stop but I also wanted to curl up in a ball under a blanket and stay there forever. Wow, this was intense. I'd never felt anything like it. I'd come to know this feeling well throughout this relationship. I re-entered the house, but I wasn't sure what to do now. It was late, and I had nowhere to go and no one to go with anyway.

The Reprise

I couldn't help myself. I needed to know what had gone wrong
– what I had done wrong. I so desperately wanted Sam to
forgive me and keep being my boyfriend and so as soon as I
got home, I was going to call him. I didn't know what on earth
I would say, and I didn't even bank on him taking the call.
Sam lived with grandparents, and they had a landline phone
in their living room. The chances of them not being in and
listening in to his call were slim, but I needed to hear his
voice. As early as I could the next morning, I walked to the
local bus stop. Thankfully the party was in a house that was
on the same bus route to my home. The bad news was that
busses were every hour on a Sunday. When I arrived at the
bus stop, I checked the timetable. The next bus was 10.36. It
was now 9.38. I missed the bus by 2 minutes! I really felt life
was being purposefully cruel to me now. There was nowhere
to sit either. My stomach was not in good shape. It brimmed
with anxiety. If I thought about it, then I seemed to encourage
more flip-flopping of my stomach, which gave rise to waves
of nausea. I resigned myself to thinking about what I'd say to
Sam once I got hold of him. I rehearsed 100 different
scenarios. Some even made me cry while I stood waiting. The
main road was empty. Every now and again a car would drive

past. I checked the timetable several times in the hope I'd read it wrong. Indeed, I had. The 10.36 bus actually was the bus that turned from Steeton to Silsden, and not the one I wanted which continued on to Skipton. This meant I'd have to get off before the bus turned towards Silsden and complete a 20-minute walk. Could my weekend get any worse I wondered? A small beige car pulled over, its indicator blinking. It reversed back towards me.

"Do you want a lift?" the driver asked.

I recognised the man. He was in his early forties and lived a few doors down from me.

"You're Tracy's friend, aren't you?" he said with a smile.

I don't know why, but I felt uncomfortable, he gave me the creeps. Even when I'd seen him on the street walking his dog, I had crossed the road to avoid him. But right now I wanted to get home. So I smiled and responded.

"Yes."

He leant over and opened the passenger side door, and I climbed in.

"What are you doing here at this time?" he asked.

I explained I had been at a friend's party and was making my way home. We chatted. He told me that he was going to Silsden so he would drop me at the bus stop. When we pulled into the bus stop, things quickly took a turn for the worse. As I began to unclip my seat belt, he leaned over to me. With a smirk, he placed his hand on my knee. He started to move his hand towards my crotch. The image of his smirky face will be forever etched on my brain.

"I'm sorry I couldn't take you home, but I would like the opportunity to go all the way with you next time. You're a very pretty girl, Natasha."

50

I was frozen. I was unable to process any thought in my head. I disassociated with my body temporarily. I don't know how I got away and out of the car but the next moment I was standing on the pavement. I saw his vehicle move back onto the road and leave. It was a small beige coloured mini metro which was a very popular car at this time. This car would make the rest of my young adult life a misery. As I walked along the main road, I was still in shock. I felt numb all over. I kept interrupting the numbness with inner monologue.

"No that just didn't happen, I must have misheard him," I said.

But then I'd feel his hand on my crotch, and I gagged. I just wanted to be home now. I just wanted the last 24 hours to not have happened. I got home, and there was now only one mission. Call Sam. I dialled his number. My stomach flip-flopping. Someone picked up the receiver.

"Sam?" I asked.

"No, I'll go get him."

The next few minutes felt like hours. The 'feeling' was back in my stomach but to add a new twist to it, it was also in my throat. "I could be sick at any moment," I thought.

"Hello," came a voice from the phone.

"Hello…it's Natasha," I said in a hushed and apologetic voice.

"Hello," said Sam in an equally quiet voice.

The conversation was stilted as I couldn't really find words, and neither could he.

"Well, I have to go," he said. "I've got my mates arriving in a few minutes."

"Oh…OK. Will I see you next Saturday?" I asked tentatively. *Please say you will,* I begged the universe.

"I don't know yet. Maybe." With that, he put the phone down.

Boom! There was that feeling once more. Evermore intense. I sat silently at the end of my bed. Still trying to understand what had happened. I had never felt as sad as I did at that moment in my life. I could feel tears rolling down my cheeks now, and I began to sob. The type of sob where your chest hurts, but you make no sound. I'd not experienced loss but I knew that this felt worse. It felt like I'd lost everything. The week ahead passed slowly. My best friend at school Annie was on hand to console me. She used all the right platitudes 'he doesn't deserve you | he's a loser | he'll regret it' but, of course, what I wanted to hear was 'He'll explain everything, just wait and see | he still will want to be your boyfriend' or variations on this theme.

Saturday night rolled around eventually, and Sarah and I were ready. Ready to meet our fate. It was 8.30 pm, and as usual, we had gone to The Grinning Rat. The usual sea of faces greeted us as we got our drinks and joined the noise. Luke was out, and he looked good. I decided I'd go over and say hi. I'd not seen him in a while, and I could use the distraction. As I got closer, I could smell him. He always smelled so good.

"Hmmm, you smell good."

As usual, Luke blushed and didn't know how to respond. He couldn't even meet my gaze.

"You always smell nice, Luke. What is it you're wearing?" I asked, now trying to normalise the conversation.

"Err, Polo by Ralph Lauren," he said awkwardly.

"Well, it's very nice," I said in my best grown-up voice.

Like I was telling a child that his crap painting was in actual fact a masterpiece. Trying to be encouraging and less assertive. Anyway, it worked. We started our usual pattern of conversation. He said he'd seen me with Sam over the last few months. I gave him a weak smile. What was I supposed to say?

"Yes, we've been hanging out a little."

Why did he have to mention Sam? I'd been distracted for the last half an hour.

"Why did you mention Sam?" I asked.

"He's over there," he responded and nodded in his direction.

My heart pounded. I turned slowly to see where Luke had motioned. There he was. He looked so beautiful. His freshly washed hair curling up on top of his shoulders. His tallish frame above the heads of his friends. He looked up, and we looked at each other. It was fleeting, and then he carried on talking to his friends. I took this as a sign. He hadn't held my gaze. He hadn't instantly come to find me, nor was he making excuses to leave his group of friends. It was over. My feet immediately took over, and I found myself in the toilets. Girls were buzzing around me, touching up their make-up or chatting. I couldn't form a single clear thought. What was I going to do? *Should I leave?* I wondered. Sarah was suddenly at my side.

"Hey Nat, I saw Sam in the pub. Has he spoken to you yet?"

I couldn't speak. I just shook my head and held the tears back.

"OK, Nat, stay here."

With that, she was gone. I knew Sarah's steely stare meant one thing. She was off to confront him and possibly tell him what she thought of him. Things were about to get worse. Moments later she was back in the toilets with me.

"Nat," she called.

I looked up, and Sarah was standing in the doorway.

"Sam is here and wants to talk to you."

My heart began to palpitate very fast. What was he going to say? *He's probably just going to ask me to call off my guard dog and leave him alone, but at least he'd talk to me,* I thought. He was standing in the passageway looking at the floor. As I walked towards him, he looked up, and our eyes met. We found a space in the passageway and Sam then proceeded to be exceptionally sweet. He explained everything to me telling me about how nervous he had been too that night. How he'd been a little too over-excited and had 'finished' before we'd actually started and was embarrassed. That he was supposed to be the experienced one but that he'd not delivered on the night. He explained that he was so ashamed that he'd run. It was a very real and honest conversation. He said he'd really struggled to come out that night as he assumed I wouldn't want to see him again and that he would be devastated if I wouldn't give him another chance. I was aghast. The very thought that I wouldn't give him another chance was so foreign to me. Of course, I was giving him another chance!

What I learned through this relationship was that I have a predisposition to giving out many more chances than people deserve. However, on this occasion, he really deserved it. The surge of feeling I now had was different, it was warm, and it engulfed me. I was 'loved up'. This was what all the fuss was about, I thought. I was in love. Yes, this was love, and it would cost me more than it would reward me in the long run – but for now, I was enjoying a well-earned reward.

Later that week, I asked my parents if Sam could come over. They'd agreed he could and so that Wednesday I decided to meet him off the bus. I lived 11 miles away from him and this would mean he needed to take 2 buses. His bus pulled in at 7ish and I was there to meet him. My mum and dad had agreed to meet him, but they were going off to meet their friends. We didn't have a 'talk' as my parents are way too cool to have needed to do that. They trusted me to be sensible all my life and this was not any different from a situation to them. We'd discussed the birds and bees when I was about 12.

They said hello to Sam and left. It was all very cordial and pleasant. We had the house to ourselves. This was going to be the night we finally did it, and we both knew it. We made small talk for approximately ten minutes and then entered my bedroom. Perfect. I knew this environment, I understood the lighting well. All went to plan – no hiccups or issues. No fireworks either, just a sweet and tender evening. We were definitely a couple now. We laid on top of my duvet and cuddled. Possibly the perfect first time for any young woman (albeit it was now my second attempt).

As we lay in embrace Sam told me about his childhood. He had a brother and a sister, both were younger. His sister had been knocked down in a fatal car crash and had died at the tender age of 13. It was too much for his parents to cope with and so they divorced. His dad had moved to London and was now not in the picture and his mum had remarried to a man who owned a factory in K-town. They'd moved to Leeds but Sam had wanted to stay at his school to take his GCSEs. The only way he could continue with the plan was if he was to stay with his very old grandparents. They'd reluctantly agreed and had made it clear they were too old to have a young man living a young man's life with them for long. He'd failed his GCSEs and whilst he figured out his next move, his new step-dad had given him the graveyard shift at the factory. Checking the machines during the night when they needed feeding with stock. Sam talked really enthusiastically about becoming an engineer and how this would be good practice for his longer term career plan. Most K-town's youths fell into engineering jobs like this one, checking and maintaining manufacturing machinery.

Several weeks passed and all was well. Inevitably as all couples do – we had our first fight. We had been in the Grinning Rat together and after 30 minutes or so I had noticed Sam's absence.

"Where is Sam?" I asked Sarah.

"He's talking to some girl in the passageway," she said, raising an eyebrow.

"He's been talking to her for over half an hour," she added.

Her words and her tone brought panic into my chest. I needed to investigate and fast. So I made my way to the passage, which connected the pub to the club. I could see Sam leaning on the wall. I couldn't see the girl's face but I could see she had long thick black curly hair and was holding a bottle of larger. Sam was smiling from ear to ear. I could see he was laughing, talking and pushing his locks repeatedly behind his ears. Just like he had done when I first met him. He was flirting with her. I couldn't believe my eyes. I thought I'd just watch for a few more moments as perhaps I was mistaken. Surely, I must be mistaken? I then saw the mystery girl raise her hand and push Sam's hair behind his ear and as she did, he grabbed her hand. I saw him lean into her and they started to kiss. I was triggered with rage. Holding my pint of cider I ran over and brought the pint glass down on the back of her head. Feeling the glass in my hand break registered my actions and in utter panic and shame I ran. I ran from the club, I ran along the main road and I kept running. I ran for 30 minutes before I made it to Beechcliffe which is a village on the outskirts of K-town. It was about 2 miles away. I'd made good time. I was so breathless now and I could feel my asthma burning in my chest. The pain within my chest broke my dissociation. I had been totally absorbed in my head. There were no thoughts, no inner voice monologue. It was like my mind had been reset to factory settings. What had I done? What the actual fuck had I done?

I met Sam the next day in town. I had rung him that morning ready to plead forgiveness. I had wanted to hear him tell me he wanted to be my boyfriend still. I wasn't interested in hearing if this girl was OK, I didn't care. I just wanted him to forgive me. He had agreed to meet me with one caveat – I came with his music tapes – I knew this meant it was over. We met in a local café in the town centre. As I arrived and entered the cafe I scanned the room. He wasn't there. My mind was still blank, there was no activity in my head, I felt empty and numb. I wasn't sure how I even got to the cafe. My numbness was interrupted when I saw Sam enter the cafe and he saw me. He sat down not making eye contact.

"Here are the tapes you asked me to return." I slid them across the cafe table. It was a cream coloured Formica table top. There seemed to be remnants of sugar on its surface. I could feel the cassette case crunching through the sugar.

He picked up the tapes and checked each case in turn.

"I suppose I should ask if that girl was alright after I left," I said sullenly.

"Maria, she wasn't OK, actually. She was really upset as some mad bitch smashed a pint glass on her head!" he said angrily.

"Did you tell her that the mad bitch was your girlfriend?" I said with vitriol on my tongue.

"She knows you are my girlfriend."

"If she knew that then why did she kiss you? If you knew you had a girlfriend, why did you kiss her?"

I was pleading with the universe that there would be a satisfactory answer to my question when I asked him this.

"We've known each other a while, we sometimes go to gigs together. We were just talking about the fact that the Ramones are coming to Leeds and discussing if we should go. We then just started to kiss. It wasn't planned or on purpose."

He said this in a pleading tone I noted. We continued to talk. My motives were clear in my mind, I needed to keep him talking until he talked himself to being my boyfriend again. That was the only outcome I would accept. We sat for nearly two hours and chatted about nothing and everything. I sensed he wanted to leave a few times but I managed to convince him to stay talking. I wasn't able to make sense of the conversation, was he staying talking because he too wanted to work through this or was he just unable to escape?

"So is that it?" I eventually asked.

"Well, I guess so, I mean clearly you can't trust me."

"But I want to trust you again, Sam, I do. I guess it will just take time."

"How much time?"

"I don't know, why are you in a rush? Has Maria given you a better offer?" I ask annoyed.

"Hey, why don't we leave the cafe and go for a walk? I have to start my evening shift in 20 minutes so why don't I show you the factory?"

I couldn't think of anything less I wanted to do. I was processing so many conflicting thoughts, feelings and messages and felt out of control. The physical manifestation of this tight pain in my middle stomach, inability to process present conversation and nausea. I didn't recognise the girl I'd become. Last night I'd hit another person with a pint glass. If someone had told me Alan had done this, I would not have been surprised, but this was me. I was capable of that behaviour. I'd felt rage, jealousy and envy such that I'd had a fight reaction. I'd never had that reaction to anything before. Then I recalled Lisa and the bottle of cider. *Maybe I have an anger problem?* I thought.

When we got to the factory, it was all locked up. Sam took pride in showing me his big bunch of keys that he had been responsible for. He opened the gates and door and let us inside. It was a small factory with one major press. Sam showed me how he fed it with plastic and it stretched the plastic to make clear polythene, which was then cut into bags. It was interesting to see the process.

"Do you trust me yet, Nat?" he asked.

"No, not yet."

"Can I kiss you?"

I wanted him to kiss me but I felt riddled with anxiety. Paralysed even. *Is this the right thing to be doing? In less than 24 hours I have physically assaulted another human and begged my cheating boyfriend to take me back. Who am I?*

"Can I kiss you, Nat?" he persisted.

"No, not yet. It's not right."

"How about I kiss you, but not on your lips?" He had picked up a polythene bag and had put it up to his lips.

"OK then."

He put the bag onto his lips and kissed me on my lips through the bag. It was a very tender moment. The pain in my stomach and the anxiety that had made my bones rigid felt better. I felt better.

Glastonbury

True to his word, Sam bought us tickets for Glastonbury 1993. £58 for the entire weekend. I didn't know how I'd ever pay him back, but I was not going to miss out on this. He'd masterfully organised the tickets and the National Express that would take us to the festival. He'd borrowed a tent and sleeping bags and some cooking equipment too. The day of the trip we turned up to the National Express station. The coach travel was a toil and a half. It was a scorching day, and there was no air conditioning on the coach. Smokers were allowed to smoke on the coach too – which was a real torment for someone like me, with asthma and a non-smoker. I made certain that those smoking knew I objected by being a bit theatrical with my arm waving around when people lit up around me.

Sam was curiously quiet on the trip, 5 hours of sitting next to virtually a mute. We both wore earphones and listened to the tapes we'd packed, and I would occasionally pass opal fruits to Sam. When we did finally arrive, it was all a bit overwhelming as there were literally hundreds of coaches and people spilling out of them. The atmosphere was palpable as people were all eager to get their luggage from the coaches and get into the snake like queue, which was the biggest I'd ever seen. I was very anxious about the queue. How long would we be forced to stand in the blazing heat to get into the event? I didn't want to appear uncool or a burden, so I kept smiling at Sam as if to communicate all was well. I noted he did the same. The excitement and nerves rendered us speechless. Everyone around us seemed to be in large groups, pulling wagons of booze and waving telescopic flag poles. They just seemed more ready than us two. Instead of feeling like we were on a romantic getaway, it felt like we'd stumbled into a party, where everyone else knew the rules of conduct and each other. We queued for a couple of hours but finally made it through the security and were on our way to experience Glasto. Sam seemed to have started to relax now and said he knew which field we were heading towards.

"We are going to this field – field 4," he pointed at our map.

It seemed like an awfully long walk to get to it with many other perfectly good camping fields before it.

"Why don't we just get to the nearest one, Sam?"

"I agreed I'd meet up with Ellen and her friends on that field."

Ellen was one of Sam's friend of a friend, and I didn't know her well. Crossing my mind as we walked in the 100 degree heat was:

a) when had Sam seen Ellen to arrange this?

b) and why had he waited till now to share this news with me?

"When you did you see Ellen and arrange this?" I spurted out.

"While you were at uni, we hung out some nights and smoked weed." He responded nonchalantly. Not making eye contact.

This was very definitely news to me! Since when did Sam smoke weed? He knew my position on drugs. I am a staunch advocate of just saying 'no'! I'd never done drugs in my life. I was petrified of doing any type of drug fearing that I'd end up a fatality statistic.

"Since when do you smoke pot?" I snarked.

"Every day, Nat, I just don't smoke it when I'm with you," he stated matter-of-factly.

I felt so betrayed. How could he be a frequent pot smoker and I did not know this about him?

"So are you meeting Ellen to smoke weed then, is that going to be my weekend, watching you and Ellen get high?"

"No, but I've got weed, and I'm selling it to Ellen and her friends to pay for this weekend," he said, his comments completely loaded with guilt.

Well played, Sam. So now I'm being asked to be grateful that you not only smoke weed but are a dealer – so that I can enjoy Glastonbury. Unbelievable.

We found Ellen and her friends, and Sam disappeared into one of their tents. I poked my head into the tent and saw Sam produce a bum bag that must have been tucked into the waistband of his trousers. He unzipped it and pulled out what looked like a brick of pot. No wonder Sam had been so quiet on the coach trip. He must've been petrified of being caught with that much gear on him. No wonder he couldn't speak the whole time we were queued up. I felt so angry. He'd jeopardised our entire trip for this. Ellen sensed my annoyance.

"Hey Nat, I brought some home-baked brownies. Would you like one?"

"That's kind of you Ellen, yeah sure," I said.

She handed me a heavy oblong Tupperware container filled with delicious looking brownies. They were massive, like small individual cakes which should have been cut into 4 normal size pieces. I'd not eaten anything since the bag of opal fruits and was pretty hungry. I took a bite and noticed she was watching for my reaction so I gave a polite smile.

"Mmm yummy, thanks."

I'm not actually a fan of brownies or chocolate cake. I can eat chocolate all day long but the cake seems to destroy the integrity of the chocolate. This tasted OK, but it had a weird chocolatey taste – but needs must. Sam suggested we go and explore the miles of festival fields. This was an excellent idea and would mean we could be on our own. There was something about Ellen I didn't like. She was naturally very pretty, petite, intelligent, funny and smoked weed. I definitely saw her as a threat. She was always wearing a cool band tee and she and Sam could spend hours discussing music. I felt she represented everything Sam wanted, and I wasn't. I grabbed his hand just to remind everyone we were a couple and snuggled into his arm. It was seriously a pathetic move, and I felt it immediately. We continued out of the camp, where we passed large groups of excitable teens and young adults drinking and excitedly chatting to one another. Piles of alcohol strewn across the pathway as rucksacks were emptied. There was raucous shouting and laughing, coming in from every direction. I noted as we exited our camp, there was a sign that said tent camping field 4. I would be sure to remember that in case we got separated. We walked through a few more camping fields and then we began to see stalls ahead. I could smell food, and my stomach was making noises.

"Shall we stop and get some food?" I asked hopefully.

"No, not now, let's keep going as I want to get to the Pyramid stage to see it." Sam said with determination.

Reluctantly I agreed. We walked through an area that had lots of stalls selling noodles and falafels, and it all smelt amazing. There were also stalls selling clothing and other festival goodies. Then there was a field with a fair in it. Waltzers, dodgem cars, a helter-skelter and lots of traditional fair rides. The fairground was thronging. As we exited this field, we saw the first sign for the Pyramid stage. It said '3 Fields ahead'.

"Blimey it's ages away," I moaned.

"I reckon another 20 minutes' walk at least."

I was already fed up, hungry and tired. I was also feeling somewhat lightheaded. In fact, the more I thought about it, the more I realised I was feeling weird.

"I don't feel so great actually." I said to Sam whilst pulling a sickly face.

"Why, what's up?"

"I feel lightheaded, and a bit zoned out, to be honest."

Sam started to laugh at me.

"What's so funny?"

"You're high, and it's funny," he continued.

"What are you on about?" I slurred. I noted I felt a bit drunk or was it I felt a bit slow?

"Ellen gave you a pot brownie." He was still laughing at me.

"Whaaaaat! That is not funny, Sam," I slurred, and became aware that I needed to sit down imminently.

We were walking through the cinema field, and the screen was humongous. I was aware of the characters on the screen speaking, so I looked up. It was the film Singles. I knew this film. I began to sit down and could feel I was wearing a ridiculous grin. I felt giddy and yet tired.

"OK, let's sit down for a few minutes," Sam said.

I woke up in a muddle. I couldn't quite sit up as my back was stiff. I rolled over to my side and could feel the pain in my back. I must have fallen asleep on the grass. I rubbed my eyes as I couldn't quite see. It was really dark and my eyes couldn't focus. It was nearing 5 pm when we entered the cinema field, and so I looked at my watch to see what time it had gotten to. There wasn't enough light to read the watch face. The gigantic screen was pitch back. I recalled reading that films would play until 2 am and so in a confused state, I concluded it must be later than 2 am. There was a slow realisation that I was on my own. There were a few people in the field with me, talking and shouting, but no Sam. Where could he be? I got up surveying my surroundings. I could see festoon lights in the distance and so walked towards them. I left the cinema field and must have taken the wrong exit as I found myself in the Pyramid tent field. The area was home to a few party-goers, but the stage itself was dark save for the signage above the stage. What time was it? Surely this stage should have some acts still on? I wandered over to one of the men in fluorescent yellow tee-shirts who were security.

"Excuse me, what time is it?" I asked.

"It's ten past four in the morning, and I think it's not the best idea to be wandering around on your own without even a torch if you don't mind me saying so," he added.

"Yeah, I've been separated from my party. How do I get to camping field 4, please?"

"It's a long way off, and essentially you have to go back on yourself, and when you get through the cinema field, you keep going straight. Head for the funfair lights and then you're 3 fields away."

I couldn't quite get my head around it. I'd been left alone in a field, passed out on drugs and my boyfriend had ditched me. I'd now walked in the wrong direction and made my walk back to our camp twice as long. I had no torch, no weapon, no map and no clue. I was seething mad. I was going to tear a strip off Sam the minute I saw him! I stumbled across the uneven ground and after nearly 50 minutes I eventually made it back to camp and found our tent. Sam wasn't there. It was possibly 6 am now and so where could he be? I figured Sam was probably in Ellen's tent, but I was now so mad at him. I didn't trust myself if I found him in her tent. I also didn't want to deal with the fact he may have been in bed with her. *No, best just to get some rest and have it out when he eventually turns up.*

"Nat, its Sam, you OK?"

"Err, what time is it?"

"It's 11.30. I'm glad you made it back OK, Nat."

"Seriously? What the actual fuck, Sam! You don't just leave someone in the fucking cinema field on their own! You don't just leave your girlfriend who is high as a fucking kite in a field on her own. What were you thinking? I'm so mad right now!" I spitted out in quite a high pitched tone.

"I didn't know what to do cos you were so stoned that you just fell asleep. It was only 5, and I didn't know how long you'd sleep for, so I asked a couple next to you to keep an eye on you so I could go find the Pyramid field."

"Oh well, that's OK then if two random strangers agreed to keep an eye on me!" I said sarcastically.

"I came back for you about 7 to get you to go to the pyramid field to see Robert Plant and The Black Crowes, but you were still asleep. I knew that you'd understand that I *had* to see them."

"Well, you thought wrong, Sam. I don't get you! Why bring me here if you'd rather just be with your stoner friends and you think it's OK to leave me in a field?"

"It's not like that, Nat. I do want to be here with you. I don't want to spend the weekend with Ellen and her friends, but I needed them to buy the weed so that I can afford to pay for us to be here, please don't be mad at me." He said using his best pleading voice and flickering his eyelids at me.

I wanted to believe him, it was going to make it easier to get through the weekend if I did. I thought briefly about making a big deal of it, but what if he left me? I'd have been on my own, without a tent and without my coach ticket home. He also managed to pull off the cutest sorry face when he needed too.

"OK, but promise not to leave me again!"

"Of course, I won't leave you again. I am sorry."

He came in to kiss me. Sam's lips on mine made my skin crawl. I hated him at that moment. I wanted to ask him where he'd spent the night but, I didn't. It would only lead to another argument. We spent the day looking around the vast fields. Browsing the stalls and chatting to other festival-goers. We had agreed on the bands we had wanted to see and spent the day following our plan. It was a bit stifled between us, and I was irritable. Other than the fact I'd come to realise my boyfriend who I worshipped was an utter twat, I also had severe back pain. The result of sleeping on a cold, grass bed. We got back to the tent around 3 am and I was utterly knackered.

"Shall we stay up and sit outside the tent?" Sam asked.

"No, I'm knackered and want to go to sleep."

"Can I sit outside the tent and chat with our neighbours as I'm not tired yet?"

"Sam, you can do whatever you want," I said. I was utterly fed up with him now.

I awoke around 6 am. Sam was lying next to me asleep. I needed to go to the toilet, and I stank. Although I'd already determined that I would not be showering throughout the weekend, I'd have to reconsider. I hadn't planned the night I spent in the field and the day before was extremely hot. I reached for my rucksack and surmised that I'd have to make the fact I only had a hand towel work. When I got to the portaloos, the queues were humongous, and so I decided to take a look at the shower queue. It was about 4 people deep for each cubicle. I decided to get in the shower queue first as it seemed to make most sense. I was watching the females ahead and was making up stories in my head about who they were, where they were from and who they were there with. This amused me for the first 20 minutes but I soon started to get restless. In my view, each person should take no more than 5 minutes. 1 minute to get undressed, 2 minutes to shower and 2 minutes to get dried and dressed. So why had my queue not gone down in 20 minutes? My anxiety began to flare up, and

I was acutely aware that my hurry sickness was working against me now. I also still needed a poo, badly. I thought I'd have been out of the shower by now and in the loo queue. The queue finally went down to the point where I was next.

The showers were plastic cubicles with doors. There were plastic shower trays, and one of the cubicle sides had a hook to hang my rucksack upon. The shower had a proper shower head and two taps. I had genuine excitement about what was about to happen, I was about to get clean. I took my clothes off and started to turn the taps to work out the right temperature. I was really concentrating on holding in the poo now. I could feel it in my colon, pushing to get out. Nope, I would have my shower quickly and get over to the loos as soon as I could. I put my head under the shower. The water was warm but being in the open-air cubicle was cold. I thought I'd make the decision to just wash my hair as it was too cold to get in the shower. I poured the shampoo into my hand and lathered up my hair. It was now apparent I was not going to make it out of the shower in time to get to the loo. The poo was here. It wasn't going to wait a moment longer. No matter how hard I tried squeezing my bum cheeks it was here! Quickly, I decided that if I could squat over the drain hole I might be able to either pick it up and bag it or squish it with my foot down through the drain hole. As I squatted I felt the motion. It was over quickly but what now lay in the shower tray was a ruler length turd. How the hell would I get rid of this? The reality of my situation hit me. I was naked, partially wet, and too cold to get in the shower and now stood next to a huge turd! I began to cry. What was I going to do? There was a queue of people outside waiting to use this shower. My cry began to turn into laughter. Raucous uncontrollable laughter. This was not happening, right? This was just surreal, I'd finally lost the plot. Never had I ever been in such dire straits. I searched frantically in my rucksack for a plastic bag to put the turd in. There wasn't one. In fact, all I had were the clothes on my back. I'd have to scoop the poop up into a sock or socks and find a way to dispose of it. Gipping, I picked up the poop to see it breaking in two. I picked up the second part which was deceptively mushy. My tears were back. This time I was really crying. I'd have to use my knickers to clean the residue from the bottom of the tray. Could this weekend get any fucking worse?

Well, I'm happy to conclude that things got much better. I managed to dispose of the aforementioned turd without drawing attention to myself. I also managed to get another pair of knickers and socks and so life got considerably better. The weekend ended with The Red Hot Chilli Peppers at the pyramid stage. This was indeed a memorable gig. In fact, the music was fantastic all weekend, and as we sat on the coach home I reflected that I should definitely like to go again next year – with friends and not with Sam.

It Was Time to Leave

Sam and I had now been dating for three months. He came to my house twice a week and then we saw each other Friday and Saturday night. It had become quite an intense relationship, as they do in your teens. Sarah had been brilliant. She'd allowed me to disappear into the relationship and hadn't given me grief about it. In fact, on a couple of occasions, she'd let me and Sam both stay at her house when her parents were back in London.

We knew that I'd be getting my A' Levels results, and this would change our worlds. I couldn't have met Sam at a worse time. During our 3 months, I had become wilfully distracted, and my studies were significantly interrupted. Let's be honest – they were non-existent. I'd always been a top-performing student and was Head Girl. The day I got my results were a bit of a shock, to everyone. I rolled up to the school where friends were already laughing or crying as they held their pieces of paper, laying out their results. I saw Annie and she came over to let me know her results. 3 Cs and 1 B. Awesome. She had wanted to be a teacher and she now had the grades to get on to her chosen course. I went to collect my envelope. I knew it would be awful, but I secretly and naively was expecting a miracle. My predicted grades were 1 B and 3 Cs.

I unfolded the letter of award:

N – German

U – General Studies

D – Business Studies

E – Economics

NUDE – I thought. How funny.

Then the realisation began to hit me. Fuuuuuuuuuuuuuck!
I was screwed. I just kept staring at the page. No! This cannot
be right. I knew I'd taken my foot off the gas a little but
fuuuuuuuuuuuuuck!!! How was I going to tell my parents?
Well, that's it, I thought, *I'm not going to university*! I
immediately rang Sam for moral support. How was I going to
let my parents know? This was the worst fuck up in all of
history. They'd be so disappointed. I was supposed to be the
first in my family to go to university. Sam's response was
entirely unhelpful and made me cross. He simply started to
laugh.

"I can't believe that!" he laughed. "That's hilarious."

"Err, not for me," I growled.

I couldn't believe that he was so insensitive about this.
This was my life he was laughing at. Since the age of 7, I knew
I was going to university. It had been all I'd ever dreamed of.
How could he be so hurtful? *Maybe,* I thought, *just maybe
he's happy because it means I'll be staying in this dump of a
town?*

My mum and dad were super supportive of my news. Well
once they'd asked all the questions I hadn't wanted to hear
like – how did you let this happen? What grades did Annie
get? Why had I let Sam distract me? Once they asked all the
obvious and painful questions they knew that I'd be more

devastated and so were on hand to help me plan what I was doing next. The next day my mum and I went to the careers office in K-town. The woman talked about clearing, and within the hour, I had two options. York or Hull. York offered me a place as long as I retook my German A' Level. That was a simple no from me. I hated every last minute of that subject. The thought of retaking it made me feel physically ill. In rejecting this offer, I did reflect that maybe I was letting go of my childhood dreams of meeting and marrying my brilliant German doctor. Hull seemed a more straightforward option. 3 school friends were going to Hull, and so it seemed like a sign. By the end of the day, I had my place, had organised to share a house with my school friends and had let Sam know. A good day's work.

It's Life, Jim, but Not as You Know It

University was a dire departure from what had been the mundanity of my life in the small northern town. The freedom was confusing. Trying to balance the new ability to choose what to do and what not to do was actually quite exhausting. I found that I didn't like getting up for early lectures and that the sheer nonsense of being on campus for an hour then off for two and so on was annoying. I soon found a routine in sleeping through the day and having late nights. Sam would come up at the weekends, and we'd go to student nights. In one particular club called Spiders, drinks were 50p. It was ridiculous, the ability to get slain drunk for a fiver.

In truth, I was not adjusting well to university. I didn't really gel with anyone on my course. I didn't really gel with my housemates. Yes, we had gone to the same school, but we hadn't been real friends. I began to feel down and have a very low mood during the week. So when Sam came to see me at the weekend I was irritable and depressed. He tried at first to cheer me up. He told me he'd be there for me and was really sweet. One particular night in my bedroom we were talking about our future.

"Well, when we get married, we can move to Haworth if you want?"

This was so unexpected and I also realised it was unwanted. This conversation left me feeling really unattached to my life. I felt empty, void of all feelings. Although it was hard to navigate I guess I knew that if I had wanted to be married to Sam then when he mentioned it, I would've been happy – wouldn't I?

Things seemed to get better for a few months, and then I simply got bored of it all. This was just about the time my grant started to run out. *Right,* I thought. *Time to get serious.* I began to try harder at classes and mobilised my lazy ass to get a job at Spiders nightclub. I got to know some of the crew at the club, and they got paid cash in hand, plus they paid for a taxi to collect you and take you home. The only fly in the ointment was Sam. Was he prepared to come over at the weekend and enjoy the club without me?

He used to come over to Hull by train on a Friday night, and we'd spend the evening catching up and watching TV and snuggling. Saturday would be the usual wander around the City's record stores looking for vinyl. Then I'd get ready for the taxi at 8 pm and see him at 10.30 pm. All was going well. Late in the semester, I decided to take a night off work so that we could enjoy a night out together. Surprisingly Sam didn't seem that animated by the idea.

"I thought you'd appreciate me taking a night off?" I quizzed.

"I'm not bothered either way," he'd said.

"Why? Why are you not bothered?"

Shouldn't my boyfriend of nearly a year be bothered if I have the night off to go out with him? I thought.

"Well, it's not like we don't see each other during the evening, is it?" he said with disinterest. I really didn't know what to say to that, but it left me feeling icky.

We went to Spiders, which isn't a massive club, but it has specific characteristics that make it very unique. It has a range of small rooms interconnected by narrow corridors. There are areas surrounded by ironwork spiderwebs which create intimate spaces. There are three main bar areas. I worked in what was known as the back bar. We headed straight to it. The unwritten rule between employees was that when you were off duty, you were hooked up with extra-large shots or cocktails for free. We offered a fabulous range of drinks with unusual names like:

- Tizer (which tasted like Tizer pop, but were lethal)
- Pink Pugsleys which were strawberry milkshake with vodka and grenadine
- Brandy Bomber – a mixture of chocolate milk and brandy
- Willy Worms which were probably our most popular drink. Cider with vodka and blackcurrant with a jelly worm in the bottom of the glass. The worm would absorb the vodka and be super squishy by the time you got through the cider.
- Tarantulas which were Pernod and blackcurrant in a pint of cider (my personal favourite).

I knew all the crew, and so we hung around the bar to chat with them. The bar was also opposite the dance floor. Sam every now and again would rush off to dance to a song. Later, I was amid a conversation with Kate – the bar manager, when

I realised I was very, very drunk. I'd gone past fun drunk to frazzled drunk. To the type of drunk where you just want to go home to bed. It also dawned on me that I hadn't seen Sam for quite some time. Possibly half an hour. I couldn't say if I'd noticed that the music had been his type of music, and he'd been dancing on his own for 30 minutes, but it didn't quite seem right. I walked over to the small dance floor. It used to become packed, and so it's not immediately obvious who is on it. It's also a dimly lit place, and so you have to enter the dance floor and manoeuvre around it to be sure of who is on it. I really didn't want to join the drunken hoards all singing along to James and 'Sit Down'. I also knew that this was not a tune that Sam would dance to. So where was he? There was an upstairs at the club too. It played 70s funk – which neither of us liked. However, they did serve food upstairs and so maybe he was upstairs having a burger? I searched around the upstairs floor but couldn't find him. I was worried about it, where could he be? I went back down to the bar feeling both tired, anxious and puzzled. As I approached the bar, I could see Sam there. He was leant on the bar talking to some pretty girl. Tall, slim and long blonde hair. I felt more bothered now than I did before.

"Sam, where have you been, I've been looking for you everywhere. You've been gone ages!" I said with some venom.

"I've been looking for you too."

"I want to go home," I pouted. "I've had too much to drink, and I don't feel very well."

He looked at me and very matter-of-factly responded, "You go home then. I'm going to stay."

What? What was he saying to me? No – that's not how this works. He was my boyfriend. If I wanted to leave, then he should go with me, right? That's how this works. I must have been pulling a face as I processed what he was telling me – that he wasn't tired. He went on to say to me that he'd not be able to sleep and that he'd keep me awake. So somehow, he was doing me a favour? He walked me to the exit and said he'd share a taxi back with my two housemates who were also in the club. I was so tired and unwell I reluctantly agreed.

I don't remember putting myself to bed, but I must have as when I awoke, I realised I was alone. Sam was not next to me. Where the fuck was he? I really didn't feel well, but I was super confused. *Maybe he slept on the communal sofa,* I wondered. I went downstairs and checked the living room. No. He wasn't there. My housemate came downstairs behind me.

"Morning," she said, way too perky for a Sunday morning.

"Jill, have you seen Sam?"

"Err, no," she responded.

"Well, did you share a taxi with him last night?"

She shook her head.

"Well, where is he?"

"I don't know," she responded.

Ian entered the kitchen. Ian and Jill were boyfriend/girlfriend.

"Ian, did you see Sam last night?"

Ian smiled. An expansive and mischievous smile. *What's he smiling at?* I thought.

"Yeah, I saw him."

"When?"

"At the end of the night, he was getting into a taxi with a girl."

So after intensive enquiry, I learned that Ian had seen Sam get into a taxi with a tall, slim blonde girl. That was at about 2.30 am.

Too Scared to Be Alone

I had let Sam give me some cock and bull story about how he'd missed my housemates, and the blonde girl had agreed to let him stay on her communal sofa. I don't think I ever really believed him, but I wasn't prepared to be single, alone or without him. Over the coming weeks, Sam became even more distant. In truth, I'd had a bit of a wandering eye too. In fact, I may have, sort of, been on a couple of dates. OK, judgy McJudgy pants – I know I'm not looking too good right now either. However, long-distance relationships – before we had mobile phones and texting – was hard work. You had to go to a public phone box with a heap of 10 pence's and get in the queue of students all ringing up their parents. One horrible autumnal evening I queued in the rain to call him.

"Hey, Sam, It's me."

He said that he had something to tell me.

"Go on then," I goaded.

"I've been seeing someone else," he said apologetically.

My head felt fuzzy, and my heart felt like a lead weight in my chest. I also had instant nausea. How was this even possible?

"She's called Harriett. She's sitting her A' Levels, and we've fallen in love. Not like us – this is real love. I've met the love of my life. We've been seeing each other on and off for about 6 months."

I don't really recall saying anything. I was stunned. Not only had I been dumped, but Sam had been cheating on me for 6 months, and he was now in 'real love'. I don't really remember placing the receiver back on the phones cradle. I remember it was late, as I stepped out of the phone booth I was surprised by how cold the night air was on my face. The road was well lit by takeaway shops lights, and people were milling about. I'd just had my heart torn out of my body and yet no one looked alarmed. I was holding my breath, albeit I don't know why. I could sense the pain in my stomach returning, a physical aching so bad that I could double over. I walked back to my house and let myself in. I made it to the bedroom, but didn't turn the light on. I fell onto the bed and curled up in a ball, to try and hold my stomach and the pain that was in it. Tears were now running down my cheeks, but I was resolved not to sob. If I started sobbing, I knew it would never stop. The problem is you can't dictate when you sob or do not sob. Sobbing I feel is the manifestation of our soul's pain. So I sobbed. I sobbed for several hours, in fact. Not moving. My candlewick bedspread had caught my tears and leaked them through to the mattress. I wanted to scream out, I wanted to talk to Sarah but I also wanted to be alone. I was so hurt, like a pain that was so deep I knew I'd never get over it. It would leave a scar upon my soul so deep, like a keloid flesh scar. It would never heal and I would never get over this. In part because I would never want to and in part because it would be impossible.

Now, this is pretty pivotal to what is about to happen in the next 20 months for me. I already had zero confidence with men, coupled with abandonment issues. Now I developed a distrust. Ironically, not with men – but with trusting my own feelings. How could I have poured love into this relationship? It may not have been real love for Sam – but it had been for me. Or at least I thought it had been as I had no other reference. This had been real love and for Sam to introduce such doubt in my mind was heart-breaking.

I went into a deep, deep depression. I didn't go out for 12 weeks. Not even to work. I missed coursework. I didn't call home. I struggled to get out of bed, wash, bathe or get dressed. Funnily enough, I did seem to be able to make it to the fridge regularly! Eventually and before I knew it, we were heading into the Easter holidays. That signalled a 5-week break from university. I had moved through the grief stages – Disbelief, bargaining, and was smack bang in 'angry' now. I went home, and I was steaming angry!

How dare he cheat on me!

How dare he go out with some youngster still doing her A' Levels! How dare he be in 'real love'!

Thankfully Sarah was on hand and helped me get my job back in K-town for the 5 weeks, and together we clocked up a lot of time talking about what a real scumbag Sam was. Of course, I quizzed her hard on why she hadn't seen Sam with this perfect girl. Surely she must have seen them together? Of course, she hadn't as he'd been secretly seeing her during the weeknights and seeing me on the weekends. I'm a dweller; actually, I'm an obsessor. So to me, the logistics of this affair was a priority in my mind. How the fuck was he ringing me during the evening and seeing her? How did he square it off with her? Was she in on the deception? I felt like a fool. I was ashamed that I had been so easily hoodwinked. That I had allowed him to gaslight me for so long without any resistance. They both must be laughing hard at my expense right about now :(((((((

The first Saturday night back in the old town felt different. All my old sixth form friends were back in town too. I'd now have to tell them that Sam and I were over, this filled me with dread. To my surprise no one asked nor cared. This hurt. Why when your world has stopped spinning, you're filled to the brim with pain and shame and not one other person notices? In fact, not one other person even thinks to enquire? This allowed me to focus on my next biggest fear which was seeing him or seeing him with her. I'd visualised losing 3 stone and going home looking super-hot. Oh, how he'd rue the day he crossed me. In truth, I'd eaten my sadness and was at least a stone heavier. We went into the pub, and I scanned the premises quickly. There was no sign of him but the tension in my neck, shoulders and head never dissipated. Over the entire 5 weeks, I didn't see him but my body couldn't relax. I was hyper-vigilant. I was exhausted by the time I returned back to uni.

You've Got to Be Kidding Me!

The weeks at uni dragged until eventually I was back in my hometown once more. Working in the local factory for the summer vacation which wasn't great but it certainly was a distraction. It employs hundreds of staff and over the summer to keep production going, it hired students. I'd met some new people from different schools, and many became summer friends. One, in particular, was called David. He was from the same village as me but had gone to a different school. He was super lovely, which I know is an overused word, but for David, it was very apt. He was over 6 foot tall, blond hair and blue eyes. I wasn't instantly attracted to him as I have a thing about good teeth. David's were really white but they were a bit crooked, somehow they were cute. I soon discovered that he came from 'good stock' which explained his almost Etonian accent. Over the summer, we worked closely and I got to know him really well. His personality was amazing. He was funny, lightning fast banter and he liked to listen. This had helped me form a crush on him. Of course, this meant I was beginning to struggle to talk to him or look him in the eye. We'd been super chatty all summer, giggling and sharing lunches most days.

We worked on piece-rate in the factory, and he over delivered every day against his target. He'd put my sticker on his extra boxes so I could get a bonus too. Every day was heaven as I enjoyed his company so much. He knew just how to wind me up without going too far. He'd mocked my poor storytelling, as I'm really good at starting a story and forgetting the names of the actors or historical figures that the story references. I love to begin stories but quickly lose my way once I realise I only know part of it. David found this hilarious and would finish telling me the story with the actual facts and nuances needed to make the story exciting or funny. There was a week when I got put on a solo project. It was in a different part of the factory and a five-minute walk to the canteen. When I got to the canteen in the morning to break, the other students had filled the canteen table. There was nowhere for me to sit. Each break dragged by and I felt kind of upset that David hadn't saved me a seat. Was he not watching out for me too? I then realised that I was excited to get the bus in the morning as he was going to be on it. I was equally sad when the day was over, and I knew that our bus ride home was quick and I would have to get off the bus. That week in isolation without his company helped me realise I 'liked him', and it was the day my social awkwardness reappeared in full. David suggested that after our Friday shift, we go to the Red Pig Pub.

"Mmm, yes, OK," I'd managed to say.

As we walked over to the pub, David was his usual charming self, making me laugh. We got to the pub, and he opened the door to let me go in first. He was very polite with excellent manners. His eyes seemed particularly sparkly blue that day. He'd been telling me stories across the assembly line of how he'd had a crush forever on some girl at school (we'll just call her lucky bitch), and had confessed he liked her a lot. She'd told him she was flattered, but he wasn't her type. Somehow, he couldn't quite get over this, and it had dented his confidence deeply. His vulnerability was really sexy. As we walked into the pub, I had turned to him to respond to his pity party statement with a mocking 'aww you're just so ugly and unloved' comment, and so I entered the doorway almost backwards. As I turned to face the bar, I saw 'them'. There was Sam with what must have been Harriett. Oh crap! That knotted feeling came back into my stomach. Now I have learned over the years that my stress response is to freeze.

Flight – no.

Fight – no.

Fawn – no

Freeze – yes.

David knew all about my harrowing story, and I'd shown him pictures of Sam, so he was familiar with his face. He saw my face and read the situation quickly.

"It's OK," he said. "I've got you."

I inhaled a sharp but deep breath.

"Go find a table and I'll bring you a drink."

He motioned to a table at the opposite side of the pub. I nodded. As I went to the table, my mind raced. What should I do? Anything or nothing? Acknowledge or ignore? David came back with the drinks.

"It's OK," he laughed. "You don't need to be scared of going into your local pub, it is your pub too."

He put his hand on my knee. This was so confusing to me as my stomach was processing stress and now my body was releasing dopamine due to his touch. Five minutes previous to this situation that knee touch would have been glorious. Not now. Now it felt like a runner up prize.

"Natasha," a voice spoke.

I looked up, and of course, it was Sam. He smiled a half-arsed smile and then grabbed a stool and sat down. What was he thinking? David, at this point, was now getting agitated.

"Look, mate, she doesn't want to talk to you," he said.

Now hang on, David, I thought – I was still secretly hoping for answers.

"Yeah, I get that, and Harriett isn't keen that I speak to you either, but I think you have the right to know something," he continued.

I looked up at him quizzically. I couldn't squeak even one single word.

"You should know that Harriett smashed her A' Levels."

My mind was racing. Why did Sam need to tell me that? Did he just need to let me know she was a total upgrade from me? *Cow! Bitch! Whore!* My mind uncontrollably was racing.

"Well, I told her how cool Hull Uni was and we went over together so she could have a look around. She applied and got in. So, from September I'll be visiting her in Hull every weekend." He looked very bashful.

Now let that wash over you. The love of your life has dumped you. He's fallen in 'real love' this time with a girl that is not you. He's convinced his true love to apply to the university you are at, and she's been accepted. EVERY single weekend they will be coming into the club you work at and will be showing me how much they really love each other. I was raging mad. Stifling my rage and in truth still bound in being 'frozen', I looked up and smiled.

"OK, well, it's a big place so let's try not to run into each other," I said. I was so calm outwardly, but inside I was in pain. Pure devastation.

David and I stayed in the same pub for a couple of hours. Harriett sneaking looks at me and me at her. I didn't like how this made me feel – jealous. A trait that was haunting my adult life still. It totally destroyed the mood for that evening, and I often wondered what could have happened that night had the stars aligned and we'd not run into twat face and the real love of his life. I didn't have it in me to continue to flirt with David. In fact, as I looked upon David's face, I now started to pick fault. The gaps in his teeth were simply too wide to tolerate. The crookedness of his mouth was annoying. His exceptionally posh accent sounded a bit fake. Yes, I'd gone off him totally in that instant.

I went to uni the following week, and I told my course friends the news of Sam and Harriett. They greeted the news with outrage, disgust and a little bit of mockery.

"It could only happen to you, Natasha," one friend chortled.

When the new term rolled around, I was very apprehensive. Maybe I just won't see them, I pondered. 18 thousand students study in Hull between the two universities. Why would I bump into them? Back to routine, and on Wednesday night my friends and I attended our rock night at Eclipse nightclub. It was a great night because I had a fabulous crowd of friends and we all knew how to have a good night out. We were big dancers and from 10 pm until 2 am we danced non-stop. My main partner in crime on a Wednesday night was Page. She was a Geordie girl reading Business Studies. She was small and petite with the straightest, longest honey blonde hair. She oozed sweetness and was akin to a Disney princess in her mannerisms. She was a glam rocker and wore the shortest skirts, longest boots and lots of added sparkly scarves for authenticity. She drank pints and could hold her alcohol well. She was really fidgety, always moving around, twizzling her bangles, flicking her hair and such. It used to drive me nuts but she was just a really happy person and it was infectious. We also had Phil as part of our crew. He was a year younger than Page and me and we'd met at rock night. Phil had had a crush on Page and followed her around for what seemed like months until she finally put him in the friend-zone. Once we arrived at the club we were comforted by the fact we knew all the people in there. They were our Wednesday night crew. There were different tribes of people who held court in designated parts of the club. My tribe and I had a specific area. We went to our designated area and set down our rucksacks. They were part of the 'skater girl' look I now adopted. Page motioned to go to the bar. Thumbs up from me. We chatted on the way, and when we arrived, I noticed that the bartender looked very, very similar to…no, it couldn't be? Oh, but it was. It was Harriett. She looked up and saw me too. Brazenly she bee-lined to serve me.

"What can I get you?" she asked.

A huge pint of shut the fuck up, bitch! screamed my internal voice. Well, of course, I didn't say that. I smiled as if there was nothing unusual about this, and my body went into its usual 'freeze' response. This meant I no longer could form any new thoughts. All inner systems shut down and needed to be rebooted. So primarily, I stood like a mannequin with a dumb ass smile on my face. Page ordered our cider and blacks and paid. We left the bar area. I hadn't spoken a word the whole time. Page noticing my lack of chat asked if I was OK. Very definitely not! I felt humiliated. Alone. A loser. She was petite, and I was taller than your average girl. She was a standard size, and I was a heifer. She had silky black, thick, long hair. I had limp, over-processed pink hair. She had big boobs, and I had B cups. She made me feel like crap. She was attending the University of Hull, and I was attending the University of Humberside (the former polytechnic). I was the ugly sister, and she was Cinderella.

I then felt angry. How dare she come to MY University and set up as a bartender in MY club. I wanted to – no need to get distracted. *I know,* I thought, *I'll go and chat someone up.* Anyone! In front of the bar so she could go back and tell Sam that I was well and truly over him. Totally not bothered by them one bit! So, I scanned the room feverishly. There was simply no one. Not one person I felt remotely attracted to. With rage in my heart and shame in my stomach, I feigned sickness and went home early.

That weekend I couldn't bear the thought of running into them, so I went back home to feel sorry for myself. None of my school friends would be out, but by real bestie, Sarah was there. She listened to my story and wholly sided with me. She was outraged. She knew just how to make my neurosis seem reasonable. I needed that. We went to the faithful old Grinning Rat pub. It was strange to see it without the usual holiday crowd. It was eerily quiet. I saw one of my brother's friends Dan. He'd known my brother for many years and had been an original brosette (fan of the 90s band Bros). He was a bit of a townie and not my cup of tea, but it was nice to see a familiar face. Something was different about him, though. His hair had grown long. *Curious,* I thought. I went over and sat down next to him.

"How goes it, Dan?" I said while giving him a warm smile.

He didn't speak and simply passed over one of his earphone buds to me. There was something really surreal about the situation. He looked sad. Burdened. He looked how I felt. I took the earbud and popped it into my ear. He was listening to Radiohead. This was a real surprise to me. I then noticed he was in skinny black jeans, black Dr Martens and a black jumper. *He's turned into a 'goth',* I thought. This pleased me greatly. We sat in silence and listened to the whole album. Neither one of us spoke. At the end of the album, Dan took his earphone back. He smiled at me and I at him.

"I'm going to my mate's house as he's having a party. Do you want to come?"

"Yeah, sure." I said.

I grabbed Sarah and convinced her that we should go, and we all bundled into a taxi. I have no idea where this party was, but we pulled up into a vast courtyard. It had a mini fountain in the middle of what I think was an actual roundabout. As we got out of the car, a pot-bellied pig ran across the driveway. Still not speaking, we made our way into the house. Sarah knew someone and immediately went off to chat. Dan held my hand and led me upstairs, where we found a room and began to kiss. We climbed onto the double bed in the room. It was a real musty smelling room. The curtains were not entirely shut, and the moonlight shone into the room like a torchlight. Dan opened up the duvet, and we climbed in. We continued to kiss but managed to disrobe our bottom halves. I don't really remember much. The whole experience is like a very faded photograph. I can make out shapes, sounds and smells in the memory but can't recall the actual sex. I'm not really sure what or why this night happened, but it was a genuine encounter. Two very lonely people, two sad hearts needing a connection. I think we were each other's tonic that night. After our encounter, I went downstairs to find Sarah. She smiled knowingly at me, and we ordered a taxi. I later discovered that Dan suffered from severe depression, and he took his own life twenty-three years later. That night was extraordinary but exceptional. I will never forget the connection we had without the need to talk. We just knew we needed one another. I will be forever grateful to Dan for that night.

The Virgin Run

During the summer holidays, I found a new friend to spend Saturday nights with. Sarah was now ensconced in a relationship with some loser. But she was happy – so I was pleased for her. I started to hang out with a woman named Lizzie. Lizzie was two years younger than me, but we had been to the same school. She was vivacious, fun, zany and liked alternative music. She convinced me to try further afield and go to Bradford to find my one true love. There was a dedicated rock club called Rios. We'd get the bus there and the night bus home. Perfect. She knew everyone at Rios like she was a local celebrity. I loved spending time with Lizzie as her energy was amazing. She was permanently optimistic and loved to dance, chat and be silly. Just what I needed. We took the bus week after week to Rios. I never really fancied anyone there, I liked rock music, but this was more a metal club, and so the men were a bit unkempt for my taste – a bit 'rustic' in charm for me (not much personal hygiene going on). My taste being posh, tall, blond and blue-eyed. Not many of those types of men frequented rock clubs to my knowledge.

Lizzie got off with some random bloke on the dance floor. He was with a mate who looked at me as if to say 'charming'. I smiled at him, and we started to chat. He was called Craig.

He had a skinhead and beard and wore a ridiculously long jumper and wasn't particularly tall for a bloke. As we chatted, I noticed how his eyes twinkled. *Pretty,* I thought. We got off the dance floor and went to find a seat. We talked about music which we had in common. He then told me his dad was a firefighter. So was mine. It's a real family profession, and there's just respect between families of firefighters. This news seemed to ignite an initial attraction, and we then began to flirt. Craig leaned in to kiss me. *OK,* I thought, *let's give this a whirl.*

Remember my 5 rules to the perfect first kiss? Well, this scored a big fat ZERO! It was awful. He pretty much ate my face off. His mouth seemed to be the same size as my face when he opened it. He was leaning into my face with such force my neck cricked. This was a disaster. How does anyone think that eating the front of your prey was sexy? Lizzie came over and explained that Craig's family were away and that we were going to go back to his. At the time I was living vicariously through Lizzie and so agreed. Lizzie was game for anything, whereas I was shy, reserved, risk-averse, and so following Lizzie, I felt I could expand my universe and experiences. Craig was actually very, very shy. He had less conversation than me. As soon as we got into his house, Lizzie disappeared, and Craig showed me to his room. He said I could have his bed and he'd stay in his parents' room. I was relieved but slightly annoyed. Why wasn't he trying to jump me? Was I not worth the effort? I laid there wide-awake winding myself up. How could he possibly prefer to sleep in his parents' bed than with me? We were twenty-something's with raging hormones. Was I that disgusting he couldn't bring himself to even try? The next morning, I woke to Craig's gentle voice in hushed tones asking me to wake up. I was a bit disorientated but managed to ask Craig where Lizzie was.

"She left early in the morning at around 5 am."

"Oh."

"She and Pete went back to Pete's place."

"Oh," I repeated.

"She said to tell you she'll call you later today."

"Oh!" I literally had no other vocabulary.

I was furious at her. What the actual fuck? #Girlcode. You do not leave your girlfriend in a stranger's house. Craig, unperturbed by my contorting face, went on to say,

"I'm going to do some gym work now, so it's probably best if you leave."

"Oh!!!"

I was now angry and annoyed.

"Where's your gym, is it near the bus station?"

"No, it's in my bedroom."

He pointed to a heap of equipment that I'd not noticed the night before. I turned to Craig, who I could now see was wearing a vest top and gym shorts. I could now see his very muscly torso. I soon noted that in the morning light, I could see the stubble on his head was blond too. A blond-haired, blue-eyed Adonis. Well, funny how a second look can change your mind ;) I felt very attracted to him, my body responded accordingly. Nipples erect, blood rushing to my vulva and the heavy rush of lust.

"Show me your reps," I said, giving him my sexy eyebrow raise.

He smiled coyly.

"OK."

He got on the weights bench and started to lift the weights. After he completed his reps, he sat up beaming with pride. I felt so horny, and so with purpose, I walked over to him and straddled the bench. I leaned in and started to kiss him, forgetting for a moment the pneumatic drill that was his kissing style. Once he began to kiss me, I remembered the neck pain of the night before. Quickly I switched to kissing his neck. I worked my way down his chest and began to reach for his button on his shorts. He jolted backwards.

"What's up?" I asked, feeling dejected.

"Err, nothing, it's just I wasn't expecting this," he said, blushing.

"Is that a good thing or a bad thing?" I enquired, giving him a fiendish smile.

"I've not done this before," he said.

Now Craig was 24 years old. I was slightly puzzled at his declaration, which must have shown on my face as he explained,

"I'm really shy and so have never got this far before."

I smiled. I continued to unbutton Craig's pants and keeping eye contact, I made Craig a man. He lay there, smiling. A full, broad smile. I felt satisfied, accomplished even. We kept looking at each other and giggling. We spent the entire morning and afternoon in his room. Naked. I then decided it was time that I made my way home.

"I can drive you."

"Really?"

"Yeah, no worries, I've got a Landover," he said with pride.

We got dressed and jumped in his Land Rover, which smelt of engine oil. He was happy to tell me all about it and how he'd bought it and re-built the engine. I then discovered that Craig was a truck driver. *Oh no, that will not do,* I thought. I was not going to fall for a grease monkey on minimum wage. *Stay on target,* I thought – tall, blond, German, Mensa candidate. Nobel Prize winner – not grease monkey. When I got home, Craig walked me to the door. My dad opened the door before I got to it.

"What time do you call this?"

Craig stepped in and immediately introduced himself and asked my dad if he knew his dad. Of course, he did, and that firefighter fraternity charm worked its magic. If he's the son of a firefighter, then he must be alright?

Craig rang me a lot over the next week. He agreed to drive over and go out to the Grinning Rat to meet my friends. I wasn't actually that sure I still fancied him and other than the fact we liked the same music our existence was not in any way compatible. But hey, a girl likes attention and so I was looking forward to seeing him. He drove his Land Rover into K-town and we parked up. I informed him of who he'd be meeting and what to expect. We went into the busy pub and I beamed. If only he'd been taller than me, I reflected. I'm 5' 8 tall. Craig was about 5' 6 tall. With his army boots on (fashion accessory only) it probably brought him up to 5' 7. Anyway, it was too late for regrets now. My friends were all there. One by one I introduced him to everyone. One of my ex-school colleagues came over to say hi. We hadn't spoken much over the last 2 years as we weren't close. She seemed keen to ask me how I was, and who my new man was. She then announced that she knew Sam and Harriett had split up. Harriett had cheated on him with some student in Hull and was spending the holidays in Hull with him.

Oh, the absolute joy! The absolute fucking joy! In truth, I took far too much happiness from this news. I felt engulfed with pleasure and couldn't stop smiling the most insane, full tooth grin, I must've looked like an idiot. I didn't care. I quickly grabbed Lizzie and told her. She did a little dance in the middle of the pub and we giggled like loons. Craig inquired why I was suddenly so happy, and I responded that my friend had just told me she'd got engaged. He bought the lie.

As we drank our way through the night, the most curious thing happened. Craig was hung around my neck (I was not happy about this as his arms were actually weighty) and he kept leaning in to snog me. I was doing my best to fight it off without appearing disinterested. In the corner of my eye, I spot a familiar figure. It was Sam, who was on his own. He'd obviously seen me and looked super coyish. I decided to take the high road and was immensely grown-up. **As if!** I let Craig snog my face off. An utter PDA. It was horrible. My neck hurt, my lips hurt, and I took zero enjoyment from the act, but this was too good an opportunity to waste. I'd checked in covertly throughout the night to make sure Sam was aware, watching, seething hahahahahahaha. Craig drove me home and told me I had some lovely friends. We'd agreed to go to Blackpool the next day so had gone home at a decent hour to get some rest. The next day he collected me, and I'd begun to feel a bit bad about Sam. He was obviously devastated about Harriett and recalling just how sad I had gotten was a sobering thought. A set of feelings so heart-wrenching that I wouldn't want anyone to endure.

During the day in Blackpool, I found it increasingly difficult to concentrate on Craig. The more I looked at him, the more I realised I just didn't fancy him. When he came to drop me off home, I told him that I didn't think we were a good fit. He was adequately devastated. I also told him that his kissing technique sucked and that he needed to lay off the gas, that no girl wanted a man who kissed them so hard it gave them a neck ache. It was hurtful – yes. But I like to think that the next girl he kissed benefitted from that harsh conversation.

You're welcome :)

What the Actual Fuck?

So back at uni and no love interest in sight! I got into a new routine of enjoying my nights out with my friends. However, we are somehow socially conditioned to be permanently looking for the one – right? One particular night my friend Page suggested going to a different club night. I'd heard of the club and wasn't that inspired but hey, a new club meant fresh meat.

Page and I got ourselves all made up, and with trepidation, we went to the club called Silhouettes. This was more of a specialist Indie club versus the rock and metal clubs I'd frequented. I felt uncomfortable. I didn't recognise anyone, and everyone sported Blur or Oasis tee-shirts, so we clung to the walls, and people-watched. These people were not our tribe. Late into the night, the DJ started to play a more rock orientated set. Page and I joined the dance floor to Rage Against the Machine. I took careful note of who was now on the said dance floor. A fine-looking man with waist-length ginger curls was bouncing around. *Mmmm mm mmmm. Yes, yes, yes! That is definitely my type.* I motioned to Page, who grinned. She motioned back, and there was his friend. Less tall, but beautiful long brown hair and leather trousers. I giggled. This was exactly her type. Page and I worked really well together as at no point would we ever be caught fancying the same men. We discreetly danced around them and made our best moves. We must have been so discreet that we never saw them again (well we did, but it was two years later, and that is a whole other story!).

Feeling really annoyed that our best moves had gone unrewarded we decided to drown our sorrows. Student pricing yet again meant that we were falling about drunk. My student house was less than half a mile away, and it was pretty safe at night to walk home. The club spilt outside and Page and I spotted some friends from Wednesday night's rock night. We all seemed equally relieved to see each other. We formed a considerable group and chatted feverishly to see who was out the next night. That's when I met Gary. Gary was a few years younger than me. Blond shoulder-length hair. Really cute. He was speaking, but I'm not sure I could make out what he was saying in truth. This may, of course, be as I too was perhaps a bit squiffy. The crowd began to meander down the street toward the main road, and I found Gary had taken my hand. I was OK with that. We got to the main road, and my house was just off it. Page suggested she walked with Gary and me. That was so sweet of her. Making sure I was OK. I gave her a grin which gave her permission to leave. Gary came into my house, and my room was the first room on the right as you stepped through the front door. It would have been the former parlour in the Victoria era the house was built. It was a massive room with a large king-size bed. I had the obligatory candlewick bedspread, which I thought was 'oh so bohemian'.

I'm not one for late nights and so was kind of eager to get on with the main event so I could get to bed and to sleep. We kissed and undressed. Nothing passionate and very perfunctory. We got under the covers and oh...wait... 'Houston we have a problem'. Nothing happening, nothing at all. I looked under the covers curiously. Gary was just smiling.

"Errrr, is something the matter?" I asked.

"Nah, this just happens when you're on speed."

"Oh, OK," I said.

I'd never taken speed nor been out with anyone who had, so this was new territory to me. *So what do I do? Do I keep trying, or is this it?* Sensing my puzzlement, Gary wrapped his arm around me and said,

"Job's fucked," and just smiled like an absolute fucktard.

"Well, I'm not!" I pouted.

We both laughed. Gary asked if he could stay until the morning and then he promised to repay me a visit the next night to satisfy my request to be his next job. Absolutely no issue from me. Having someone in your bed strangely filled the unwelcome feeling of loneliness and emptiness that had grown quite strong while being at university. Surrounded by literally hundreds of people every day, going to and from classes had a way of making you feel small, insignificant even. I had a good range of friends really, but I always felt that other groups of friends appeared happier or seemed to be having more fun or were just better friends.

I'd tried really hard not to be the same bossy girl I was at school, but had struggled as you can't change who you are fundamentally. I know that I come across as full-on, aggressive even, at times. I'm really not like that at all. I'm actually a painfully shy girl, who just assumes no one likes her and over tries to get people on board with my somewhat erratic personality. Being a people pleaser is exhausting though, so I tend to overdo the friendship bit and then disappear for respite and self-care. This apparently means I'm aloof. This narrative swims around my head a lot, more than it should and feeds my self-esteem low. So, when Gary asked to stay, it was an easy yes. A warm body in my bed without the need to converse or attempt to be interesting. Gary stayed and awoke early as he had to get to his job. Even better. No guilty chat. He'd left his phone number so I could queue up at the local phone box on a date of my choosing. A re-match if you will. We'll see, I lamented.

Rebounding

The following week I was looking forward to rock-night. I fancied an uncomplicated night with my friends and to spend the night dancing. The club played all my favourites, and there was comfort in knowing the faces that would appear on the dance floor with the different song choices. There was the glam metal crew who I would secretly giggle at. They were a friendly crew, but their clothing made me laugh. An abundance of skinny jeans, bandanas as headbands, wrist bands and floating scarves as they walked. My friend Page was into glam rock, and so I'd be forced to attend the dance floor to dance to songs that I actually found quite painful to listen to. Songs like 'She's my cherry pie' from a naff band called Warrant. This was anthemic, and if you liked glam music, you were on the dance floor in a shot. Then there was the death metal crew who didn't move while dancing. They had a tendency to spring onto the dance floor like 'Tigger' and then be glued to the floor with their heads down and swishing their long unwashed manes – playing air guitar. Every now and then the DJ would play a little 'Goth' section. Usually, a couple of songs and the floor was nigh on empty. I'd be there! This was my jam, and these were my songs. My friend Page would awkwardly sway as she kept me company while I sang my heart out.

On this particular evening, there was a new body on the dance floor. Intriguing. A tall willowy silhouette, with long, long black flowing hair. Black boots, black clothes. A really committed Goth I smiled a broad smile. Now, although I'm a shy type, I'm not unaware that I have a great smile. A smile that makes everyone around me smile. When I smile my wide smile at a target, invariably they are unable to not notice. In fact, it's my one and only pulling move. 100% effective to date. So I smiled at him. He smiled back. We left the dance floor, and he came immediately over to me.

"I noticed you smiling at me – was it at something in particular?"

Smart, I thought.

"Oh no, it's just nice to see another Goth on the dance floor," I replied. My teeth were now dry from smiling so intently.

"I'm Matt," he said.

"Hi, I'm Natasha."

"Which uni do you go to?" he asked me.

This was a thing in Hull. There was Hull University which was the original university and Humberside University, which was the old Polytechnic College. I'm from the latter.

"Ah, right, what is it like over there?"

So I'm assuming he's a Hull University student and not at Humberside. Those who attended the 'real uni' had a disregard for those of us not smart enough to attend the real uni, and this attitude really pissed me off. I'd go on a bit about how I wanted to go to Hull and that the original uni doesn't have a business course and so I had no choice but to go to the

Poly. This always seemed to bring parity back to the conversation. We chatted about the course he was doing, which was forensic science. He was a year ahead of me, and I liked that fact. He was from Leicester, which was somewhere I'd never heard of. Somehow the conversation turned to him being new to the club.

"I've not been before because me and my ex – 'Rachel' – would have a date night on a Wednesday night."

"Ah, right, is this a recent breakup?"

"Yes. Last week, my friends dragged me out here to cheer me up," he said with a whimsical smile.

"Is it working?" I enquired with a little wink.

As he began to laugh, he nodded. "Yes, it is."

I took my drink and positioned the straw coyly, in-between my fingers and seductively slurped up liquid. I probably looked like a prat, but at that moment, I felt like a temptress. *Can I pull this off?* I thought. *Can I get Matt to move on and more specifically move on to me?* I can't describe why in 99.9% of life I'm super shy with men and then on the 0.01% of times I'm like a woman possessed. I go from feeling like a wallflower who nobody would fancy to thinking I'm invincible like a seductive vixen. Like I have the power to tempt any mere mortal with my wit and seductive skills. It's almost like an out-of-body experience. I am observing myself pull these alluring moves; the lip biting, eyes smouldering, arm touching and other moves. At the moment, I'm a temptress in control. Days later, I'll berate myself for acting like a cheap YouTube porn star.

Well, it didn't go to plan at all. I spent the next hour trapped by Matt and his incessant recollection of how much in love he was with Rachel and how he felt sure they'd find a way back together. At one point, I even started giving him bloody advice.

"Feels like she just needs some space to realise how much she misses you and being with you," I said consolingly. *WTAF?*

Page came by and asked if I was going to do any more dancing and reminded me that had been my only purpose that night. *Brilliant,* I thought. *Page to the rescue.*

"Do you like him?"

"Not bothered, Page, actually, I thought I liked him, but he's just spent an hour whining about his ex."

With that, we got back onto the dance floor and danced for the next couple of hours only stopping for loo breaks. The lights came on, and as usual, we filtered off the dance floor and spilt into the streets outside. This was a weird time of night. Not much ever happened, but we hung around for a good hour just drifting between conversations and mingling between the tribes. This was Page's favourite part of the night as she could mingle innocuously with the man of her dreams. Dan. 'Dan, the dancing man' as I'd refer to him. Dan was tall, wiry and very bendy. I know this as when he danced, he'd almost double in half as he head-banged away to the glam rock session. Dan also moved across the dance floor as if performing to an audience on Broadway. Page would literally swoon as he gyrated his hips. I'd simply laugh at her. I found him quite ridiculous like a cartoon character, but he gave Page goosebumps. I've always been intrigued at why some people find others attractive. For Page, it was his dancing moves, and she thought he was sexy as hell. This was an utter mystery to me. The crowd thinned, and I saw Matt as he saw me.

"Hey," he said as he strolled over.

I smiled back. Not my winning smile. The type of smile where your lips disappear like you're greeting someone you once met but don't know very well.

"Look," he said. "I don't think I made a very good impression earlier. I mean I didn't realise how much I was talking about Rachel, and actually, I'm not that bothered about her really." He gave me a really big-eyed sorrowful look.

"That's OK, breakups are hard, and it sounded like you were really in love."

This comment stinging as I recalled that Sam hadn't 'really been in love' with me.

"Well, suppose so – but actually I wanted to tell you that I really enjoyed meeting you and think you are really beautiful."

He shyly looked away after he'd deposited the comment awaiting my reaction. I smiled. My winning smile once again.

"Thanks," I said and bashfully looked to the floor.

He moved closer and put his cupped hand under my chin, he tilted my head up to look at him. Now, this was a surprising move on his part. I hadn't known how much this particular move meant to me. He'd treated me like a thing of beauty. Like the moves, you see on the big screen in a rom-com. I hadn't realised just how much I'd wanted to be treated this way. Like the pretty girl. He moved in to kiss me and a thousand thoughts went through my head:

- *I'm really not that into you*
- *You've got kind of big teeth, and they might clink mine*
- *I'd rather be in the kebab shop getting my kebab*

- *I wonder who is looking.*
- *I hope people don't think I fancy this bloke*
- *Where's Page?*

I kissed him back, I'm too polite for my own good sometimes. Surprisingly it wasn't dreadful. It certainly wasn't fanny tingling great either. It was OK. He pulled away grinning like a fool. I think his review was that he'd just landed the perfect kiss – so I smiled sweetly back. He then took hold of my hand as if we were now somehow promised to each other. I felt so bloody awkward. How could I get rid of him? I looked towards Page and using ESP screamed HELP. Alas ESP was not working that night and we walked down the avenue from the club hand in hand. He started introducing me to his friends. God, will this nightmare ever stop I thought? Thankfully, his crew wanted to go home along a different road, so we said goodbye whereupon he came in for another kiss. I obliged. I didn't want to destroy his confidence after his breakup.

"Thank fuck for that," I said to Page.

"You make me laugh, Nat," she said, shaking her head disapprovingly at me.

"Whaaaaaat?" I shrugged but smiling at the ground.

"You know what!"

I did know what, I knew that I'd told her I thought he was fugly and then had snogged his face off. The good news is I never had to see him again. Hull is a vast place and lots of students, so chances were I won't see him again. The next day I was cycling to uni, and as I waited at the crossing to let the meandering students cross, I saw him. Seriously – I did! He was one of the slow ones chatting to his friend – deep in

110

conversation. *Please don't see me,* I thought. I looked OK, it wasn't that I was looking rough after the night before or anything. I just didn't want the awkward daylight conversation. Alas, it was not to be. He looked up and right at me. It was instant recognition. Damn it! I smiled really weakly, and he motioned to meet him on the other side of the crossing. What a dilemma. The lights changed, and the car behind me beeped to move, and so I pushed hard on the pedals and motored on. Not looking back for one second. Seeing Page as I locked my bike up, I recalled the story to her.

"That's awful," she said.

"I know," I said, making a screwed-up face and laughing.

"No, I mean you! You're awful. You should've stopped to tell him you couldn't wait." She pulled this sympathetic face that made me feel a bit guilty.

"Really?" I screwed my face up again.

I did think about it more that day and the couple of days that followed and still couldn't fathom why it was so wrong to have just cycled past him? That Saturday I went to work at the club but was told I had been 'promoted' and was now to take everyone's money at the door. I had taken it badly. I'd taken it to mean that the bar staff didn't like me and had voted me out. Looking back, it was probably the fact that I was a hard worker and got on with the job and that the bar manager had recommended me for the responsibility. At the time I was sulking about it. The person who took your money on the way in was invisible. People didn't look at me, and I didn't look up at them. The pay booth was set back and low. I had to crawl under the desk to get behind the kiosk, which also had a wrought iron web from countertop to ceiling for security.

As I sat, my eye-line simply saw the hands handing me cash. Every now and again I'd recognise a person's coat cuffs and look up to say hi. Particularly I'd look forward to seeing a couple of patrons to whom I thought were 'fit as'. I'd memorised their coats and sleeves and the highlight of my long-arsed night was seeing their hands pass me their entrance fee. For those who I super crushed over, I'd wait till they had paid and were entering the club to sneak a peek. 'Covert crushing' was a skill I was actively practising and was pretty accomplished at. The night passed in the usual way. People are exceptionally habitual. I had the early crew at 10 pm. The steady eddies from 11–12 am and then the scenesters. These were those who thought they were extra cool coming in after 12. At 1 am, I was freed from my prison and went to the cloakroom. I liked the staff at the cloakroom. We would have a real giggle between 1 and 1.30 when no one really needed the cloakroom. This particular evening, I started the walk towards the cloakroom when I was intercepted.

"Hey, Natasha."

I looked around and wasn't sure where the voice was coming from. I then saw a tall, looming man a few people deep. It was from Matt.

"Oh, hi, Matt."

"You didn't meet on the other side of the crossing." He threw me a pretend cross face. This was actually kind of cute. OK, ten attractive points, Matt. Well played.

"Ah, right, yes. Guilty as charged. But in my defence, I was obstructing the flow of traffic and had a lecture to get to." I giggled.

"I didn't know you worked here."

"Well, we only really talked about Rachel, didn't we?" I said sarcastically.

"Suppose so. She's here actually. At the bar – with her new boyfriend."

I could sense how heavy his heart was.

"Oh, right. Sorry to hear that."

"That's OK," he said. Then he smiled really wide. "My new girlfriend works here."

WTAF. Errr no, Sunny Jim. That is not the case. Definitely not. Not happening. Sensing my hostile reaction, he reached out to touch my arm.

"I'm joking. I meant my pretend girlfriend," he corrected himself.

I winced and started to move away.

"Matt, I have to work so I can't have this conversation right now."

"Yeah, sure. Well, shall I wait for you outside at 2?"

Definitely not, Matt. "I don't finish 'till 3, and we get a dedicated cab home. So please don't wait."

His face fell. I felt like I'd just told him his penis was the smallest thing I'd ever seen. Embarrassed and sad in equal measures, I scuttled off to the cloakroom.

"Let me in! Let me in!" I shouted.

I told one of my colleagues, Mel, in the cloakroom what had just happened.

"Get a life," she said, laughing rather over dramatically.

That was Mel all over. Totally over the top. Very theatrical. She was a small and stout woman. Robust is how I'd describe her. She was stunning and had super cool 40s style coiffed hair. She was a local girl from Hull studying at Hull uni. I pointed him out to her.

Over there, the one leaning near the bar.

"Errrr, he's gross. I hope he's got a huge dick," she spurted.

The whole cloakroom cracked up in laughter. The queue for coats was never-ending, and we worked bloody hard behind that counter. I could see Matt in the queue and looked at Mel to give her the signal. She nodded. Perfectly timed, she reached to get his ticket. You need a good line of offence and defence in this game. Some friends who act as buffers, so you don't have to 'deal'. Alas, he leaned into the cubby hole and shouted towards me.

"Will you be out on Wednesday, Natasha?"

"Probably," I whimpered.

"Great, I'll see you Wednesday," he yelled.

Fucking A, I thought. Well, that's Wednesday night ruined from now until eternity.

Wednesday, Bloody Wednesday

Wednesday rolled around quickly. I usually looked forward to Wednesday evening rock-night at Eclipse and had an entire routine to get ready. A nice long shower, shaving legs and armpits, squishing and icing zits, makeup application followed by hair drying. I had long brown hair that had been repeatedly processed with bleach and I was sporting purple hair dye that week. I'd dyed it that Monday before my regional economics lecture much to my friends' amusement. The trick with these high pigmented hair dyes like 'Directions' is to make sure you wear gloves. You should also not shower the residue off unless you are prepared for your skin to be dyed too. I'd not worn gloves, and I had showered. My neck and hands were Cadbury's purple. I'd tried using nail varnish remover to clean it off, it hadn't worked. I then tried bleach. That had burned my skin but not removed the purple. In the end, I gave up and just cycled to uni in the hope no one would notice. They did! As I got ready, I played little conversations over in my head. I knew that these conversations would definitely not be had with any of my hot crushes. Not tonight. Tonight, I was dreading it. How could I let Matt down gently but enough so that he'd get the message?

Well, in a disappointing turn of events he didn't show. Bloody charming! I like to think I'm pretty straightforward, I didn't like Matt, but I wanted the right to turn him down. I appreciate this is mean, but a girl like me doesn't get many chances to turn advances down, and this was my turn. I was pretty sulky most of the night. Not really knowing why but I guess feeling rejected. He hadn't turned up so, essentially, I'd been dumped before we even started anything. Page kept shaking her head at me.

"You didn't even want to see him."

"Yeah, I know," I retorted but I felt icky.

We filed outside as we did every week and my heart wasn't in it. I just wanted to go home and sleep so that my overactive brain would shut the hell up. I motioned to Page that I was heading off. She shot me a look that communicated 'be safe', and I waved in acknowledgement. As I turned onto the main road, I heard someone shouting my name. I figured it was my friend Andy as he lived next door and probably just wanted to walk home together. I turned to greet him and was completely surprised to see Matt.

"Oh, hi, Matt," I said, genuinely puzzled.

"Hey, I saw you leave the club and thought I'd say hi."

"Oh, were you in the club?" I asked with a puzzled face.

Seriously I'd walked loop after loop of that club that night pretending not to look for him.

"Yeah, I was at the little bar in the back room. I saw you a few times, but I guess you didn't see me?"

"No, no, I didn't. Why didn't you say hi to me then?"

"Well, you were pretty clear the last we spoke that you weren't that into me, so I just kept my distance."

Eurgh. I felt icky again. I didn't like the thought of someone experiencing pain at my doing. He was already having a hard time, and somehow, I'd managed to kick him in the guts. Now you should know I'm an empath. So that means I feel things very, very deeply. It is a huge character flaw and causes no end of inner sabotage and extended dialogue. So right now, I'm monologuing how I'm an evil human being as I've hurt someone who actually seems OK and doesn't deserve my battering. So maybe I throw him a bone?

"Don't be daft!" I said with indignation. "I just can't flirt while at work. They watch us like hawks and besides I don't want everyone to know my business."

With that last sentence, I shot him a slightly devilish 'come hither' look. Crikey, quick as a flash he's next to me going in for a kiss. *Well, I may as well,* I think. After what was a very enjoyable seg-way I'd changed my mind. Fickle, you say? I couldn't agree more. Suddenly, Matt appeared more handsome than I remembered. This is a typical reaction from me. Give me alcohol and a good kisser, and I'm anyone's. With a coy grin on my face, I enquired, "Do you want to walk me home?"

We both knew I wanted more than an escort home, and he quickly nodded. Hand in hand, we walked along the roadside. I can't recall what we talked about. It wasn't necessary. In my head I'm now going through the sequence of manoeuvres I'll need to make it so that I'm seen in the best light. Both literally and figuratively. We ventured into my vast boudoir and I turned the bedside lamps on. These were pretty poor for lighting, which made them perfect for such events. I began to take my boots off as nothing kills the passion like waiting for someone to take their boots off. I was also aware that I was wearing 100 denier tights. I'd been dancing in them all night and so was pondering excusing myself to the bathroom so I could quickly air my bits off. Nope. He's on me. Kissing my neck. *Yes, that's nice.* Undoing his trousers. Now, this really annoys me. If I want your pants off, I'll initiate this so just slow down buddy. I grabbed his hand and gave him a look, a grin and playfully took over.

Well, it was just about average. I'd say just slightly below. Not horrible in any way, just underwhelming. Always good to have a bit of exercise, though, right? I enjoyed the spooning more that came afterwards. You can always tell when a man has been in a serious relationship before as their routines become much more palatable. A long cuddle followed by rolling over to find his own space to sleep in. It is so much easier to get to sleep when you're not wondering if they are dying to get up and leave – or if you want to get up and go. The next morning Matt and I exchanged details and said we'd see each other on Saturday. I was actually looking forward to that. Strange I mused.

That Saturday, I went to work as usual. I didn't feel apprehensive about seeing Matt, but in truth, I wasn't terribly excited either. It was like a song coming on the radio that you know all the words too. Predictable, enjoyable, but not exciting. I like to think that in the early days a relationship should give you a tingle in the tummy. It should be all-consuming where you make believe a huge range of scenarios in your head from fantasizing about toe-curling, fanny quivering sex to the obligatory wedding fantasy and kids and beyond. Matt was more like thinking about what sandwich I might have for lunch. Not even a sexy sandwich. Cheese or ham on white bread.

The night wore on, and I saw a million faceless sets of hands as I took the punters cash on the door. Curiously I was sure I saw the chap from Silhouettes. The guy with the long ginger curly hair. I only glimpsed him but not many men fit that description. I hadn't had a chance to really check him out as the doorman decided at that time to ask if I needed a drink. Always! It was red hot in my little booth. As he returned with my water, I saw Matt enter. Oh, dear god. I was no longer drunk, and he was no longer even slightly attractive. I was wincing as he came towards me with a really enormous goofy and toothy smile. I couldn't remember his teeth being so big and protruding like that before. However, the empath in me was smiling encouragingly at him. *Oh no – this is not going to work! How do I get myself into these scrapes?* I could hear Sarah laughing at me as I sat in my booth. She'd be rolling around with crinkled eyes saying something like: Gosh, Nat, you're so funny, you always do this!

She would be right. I have a knack of picking fuglies and those who are emotionally wounded. I'm just too giving, and now I will have to spend the rest of the night in my little cage wondering how to get out of this new arrangement. I refuse to call it a relationship as, after all, it had been a few casual snogs and one below-average fumble. This shouldn't be too hard to get out of, should it? Well, the answer to that, my friends, is – yes! Try as I might, there was no way of letting Matt down. I tried the 'Uni is just so hectic', and I got a response of 'I'll pop 'round and give you a massage'…and sex.

'I'm seeing a distraught girlfriend tonight and won't be home till after midnight,' to Matt rolling up at midnight and…sex.

For goodness sake, I thought, and so told Matt that I had to go home for the weekend and that I'd see him later…much, much later.

When I got home, Sarah was keen to hear all the tactics I'd tried and offered some supportive heckling and laughter.

"Thanks, Sarah, you're a real help."

"Well, you do get yourself in some scrapes, Nat."

"Yes, I do, BUT I can't help it if I'm too kind and these losers take advantage of me." I say defensively.

She was nodding, laughing and snorting at me and so I joined in. I am quite ridiculous, she's right.

The Mystery Man

Sarah, Lizzie and I decided to go to Rios in Bradford. That was a nice change of scenery for me. I had booked my work off for Saturday, and I could be the punter and not the worker for a change. Some nights at Rios were electric. Music was excellent, talent was everywhere, and you knew you're in for an adventurous night. Tonight was not one of those nights! It was dead. The music was dreadful, and the talent was at home or somewhere entirely different. So, the three of us sat and chatted. The atmosphere was dank, and all three of us were low in energy.

"God, this is bloody terrible, what a waste of a Saturday night!" I harrumphed. "I'm going to the bar to get some shots," I said with conviction.

Behind the bar was a young man with long silky blond hair. Reminiscent of a Viking. He turned to serve me, and I noted his piercing blue eyes.

Well, things just got a little more interesting – I smiled inwardly.

"Yeah, can I get three red bull vodkas, please?"

He nodded and set about fulfilling my order. *OK,* I thought. *It's time to turn on the charm, dial up the smile and start to make conversation.*

"It's a bit dead tonight," I said to him.

He didn't respond. *OK, maybe he didn't hear me,* I pondered.

"I said it's a bid dead in here tonight?"

"£9 please," he asked, holding out his hand. A rather attractive hand with long willowy fingers.

"Yeah, sure, keep the change," I said as I handed him a tenner and flashing now all my teeth.

Nothing.

Nada.

No exchange of anything.

What's happened? Have I lost my Moxy?

When I went back to the girls, I was amid sulk.

"What's up with you?" asked Lizzie.

"I just tried chatting to the barman, and he totally ignored me," I grumbled.

"Oh, that's Alex. He's just been dumped by his girlfriend. She works here in the cloakroom."

"That makes it even worse then as he should be open to advances if he's not locked in a bloody relationship."

Sensing my annoyance, Lizzie explained that he and his girlfriend had been seeing each other for a few years and so it was not a simple 'get over it' situation. I may be an empath, but I'm also a stubborn old goat. I'm a Capricorn, and we were built for perseverance. So, throughout the evening, I visited his bar several times. Each time attempting to strike up a conversation and each time failing miserably. *Never mind,* I thought, *you can't win them all.* We got on the night bus home and another failed evening. Not one bite. Humbug! Over the next few days, I couldn't get him out of my mind. He was gorgeous, and I was not prepared to leave it. I decided to write him a letter. How romantic, right?

So I Write Him a Letter

To the beautiful barman,

You served me several times on Saturday night, and every time I tried to make you smile, so I could see your beautiful blue eyes light up – but got nothing. It makes me sad to think that someone with your potential smile had such a rubbish night that you couldn't manage even one small smile.

I happen to think you are beautiful and with your long silky locks kind of looked like a strong Viking type – a silent warrior. Anyway, I'm hoping that this letter at least brings a smile to your perfect face.

I live in K-town and am a student in Hull. If you ever fancy coming over to K-town for a drink, write me back at uni and send me your phone number and we can meet up.

OK, it wasn't Shakespeare or anything, but I made my point. I sent it to Alex, using the following address.

The gorgeous blond-haired blue-eyed barman (looks like a Viking).

Rios Nightclub,
Bradford

As I posted it in the letterbox, I chuckled to myself and thought, you have to try and at least make a little magic if you want to have magic in your life, right? This view has, from time to time, got me in some right bloody pickles. There's probably a medical term for me? Someone who thinks that you can create these rom-com moments in your own life. Some may simply comment I'm a nutter or a psycho, but I like to think I'm a hopeless romantic. (Turns out its ADHD. The majority of my impulsive adventures were down to undiagnosed ADHD). A couple of weeks later and having totally forgotten about my stunt, I received post. Curious as I didn't really receive much post at uni, I wondered if it could be a letter from Alex. Surely not. Now unlike the rom-coms, I didn't skip into my bedroom and carefully slice it open. I tore it open like a fat kid eating cake. It wasn't as I imagined. I thought there might be some preamble but no, just a few short sentences.

Dear Natasha,

Thanks for your letter, it cheered me up. I'm up for a meet. My number is 07525 655475.

Righty then. What do I do with that? I tell you what I do with that...skip, jump, and squeal. RESULT! Firstly, I ring Lizzie to tell her about my stunt. Lizzie knows me well and isn't surprised at all.

"You're a nutter."

"Well, yes, but should I ring him?" I asked.

"'Course you should, when you next come back to K-town."

"Well, I can come back anytime really, when should I say?"

"Well, do it mid-week as he'll be working the weekend, right?"

"Oh, OK, yeah, sure. I can come back next week as I don't have any lectures on Wednesday afternoon."

"Cool, let me know how *the* call goes," she giggled.

"Bog off, Lizzie," I said in a mocking voice and laughed equally.

I rang him after rehearsing the conversation. Much like his letter, he's not a man of many words. Just a sequence of 'yes's and no's. We arranged to meet at the bus station at 7.30 pm (early I know, but he didn't drive and would have to get the bus back to Bradford). I'd chosen my most flattering outfit. A flared jersey red dress, black tights, para boots and black holey jumper. Remember, guys, I'm alternative, and I've put as much thought, consideration and effort into this as you might your best jeans and a cute top. God, I was nervous. Butterflies swirling around my tummy. You know where you feel sick but could quite easily be a poo coming, and you've got sweaty palms, the lot. His bus pulled up. I could see through the window that he was going to be first off. Shit. How do I greet him?

Hi?

Hello?

Coy smile?

Should I be mysterious and just sidle up to him and lock lips?

Well, it turned out I was not in my own rom-com, and when he got off the bus, he looked at me and said,

"Where's the beer then?"

"Yeah, sure, the pub is just around the corner."

I get he was nervous, but really that's the best he could come up with?

"You gonna get the first round?" he asked.

At this point, I was now regretting this entirely. He was a bit of a Neanderthal and not in a Viking way. In a moronic way. I placed the two purchased pints on the table. Mine's a pint of cider and black. As I moved to sit next to him (I read somewhere, it's more intimate if you sit side by side) my leg hit the table and my cider fell over. It travelled at lightning speed towards me and covered my dress. It then began to soak into my tights. *For fuck's sake!* Alex thought this is bloody hilarious. He must have laughed for a good 5 minutes. I attempted to make the lake of cider run away from me but had zero luck. Most notably, he neither jumped to get me napkins, nor did he jump to get me a replacement drink. So, within 5 minutes I was wondering how I could get out of this horrid date. My bus only ran every hour, and there were 45 minutes left 'til the next one but I'd rather sit with my disc-man on than be sat here now. I imagined Lizzie laughing at me.

"Nat, you're soooooo funny. This is such a Nat story," she'd be saying soon enough. She'd be right. 15 minutes before my bus, I got up and said,

"Thanks for coming and taking a leap of faith but let's face it, the reality has been pretty dire. My bus goes in ten, so have a safe trip back to Bradders."

I turned on my heels and half running, half skipping, I legged it. I went to the first bus stop out of town in case he went directly to the bus station. What a bleeding nightmare. Would this stop my hapless love of rom-coms and the thought that the cheesy 'meet-cute' stories could only exist in films? Abso-fucking-lutely NOT!

Matt Has to Go

I get home on Thursday, and I now have to find a laundrette to wash my best pulling dress. I pull together a load of washing and head to the laundrette. We had a washing machine in the house, but it had broken, and we were awaiting the landlord to arrange a fix. I didn't mind trekking to the laundrette as I'm OK with being alone. I'd take a book and my music, and I'm sorted. After loading the machine and fannying around for the right change, I watched my washing go round. In my little world, I'm wondering if some hottie might come in like off of the eighties Levis advert. However, as bad luck would have it, Matt walked past. Seeing me, he turned back and came into the laundrette.

"Heya," he said in a way which was now really irritating to me. To be honest, his existence was very annoying.

"Hi," I limply smiled.

"I just thought I'd say hi."

He turned and left. That ladies and gentlemen is the end of Matt.

Rocksoc Sucks Ass

My best friend Jane (on my course) has been wittering on about me going to the Uni Rock Society. The Rocksoc. There's something really wrong about attending the other universities clubs, imho. It made me feel disloyal, and in truth, I was embarrassed that every time someone might ask me what I was 'reading', I'd explain Economics, and they'd know that wasn't a degree at the real Uni. Therefore, I was a) a thicky and b) a fraud. Jane had transferred from a different degree at the end of year two and had sat next to me in year three. She was from Birmingham and had a thick Brummie accent. She was exceptionally clever and seriously beautiful. She was relatively tall with mousey brown shoulder length, straight hair and the palest white skin I have ever seen. She wouldn't look directly at you. She would look at my right ear lobe when she spoke. I never got to the bottom of why she did it, but she never looked at anyone directly. She had met a man in her first year (Rusty) and lived with him since the second term. She never socialised outside of university, instead choosing to travel to and from university for lectures and seminars only.

This one time, Jane had caught me feeling a little low. I wasn't upset that Matt had not been bothered to even break up properly but was upset that now there wasn't also that disaster going on. So yes – I would go to the Rocksoc, Jane. Jane's boyfriend, Rusty, went to Hull uni. He was tall, skinny and had long brown hair. He was undeniably handsome, but he knew it. He was into rock music, but Jane wasn't. In fact, she wasn't into any music and was a curious girl. If you asked her about her music choices, she'd simply shrug. In fact, if you asked her about any of her interests, she'd shrug. She was really intense despite her lack of interest in anything. Rusty and Jane's schedules clashed a lot, so she had quite a bit of free time in the day. She was the sort of friend that was low maintenance, she wouldn't want to get ready to go out together or discuss outfits. No, she'd meet me in the bar at 9 and wouldn't have changed, put makeup on, brushed her hair or done any prep work. She had an inner confidence that to this day I haven't seen before or again.

Not such a great trait for me, though, as I enjoyed the pre hustle of going out. The shower where you'd languish in the cleansing water and dream about the night's possibilities. The blow dry – you know it wouldn't go to plan, but there was always a tiny hope that the hour spent blowing out your long over-processed hair would somehow end up in a moment of pure bliss where every curl fell into place. Then you'd fight through the heat you'd now filled your bedroom with and while your face was sticky with sweat, you'd begin to apply the makeup. There were no specialist products to worry about. It was simple. Liquid foundation (Rimmel was top of the range in the nineties). Followed by lashings of concealer to cover the spots. Heavy daubing of powder to stop the shine and some Dior cream blush. There was a sense of opulence when applying the blush. Finally, the mascara and lipstick and *et voila*, I was ready.

As Jane had agreed to meet me there, it meant going into the bar by myself and hoping I'd see them. Rusty's friends were not my friends. I didn't have anything in common with them at all except Jane. Rusty was very popular, and Jane knew of his reputation, so she never left his side. Trying to be 'Mrs Entertaining' to him and his friends. She was worth a hundred of him, but he had her clearly under his spell. She drove him everywhere so he could drink. She worked part-time at the main Sainsburys, and I think she paid for their rent and food.

I arrived at the student's union and immediately felt like it was visible to everyone that this was not my union. I decided to go to the bar to see if they were there. Nope. I ordered a pint of cider and black. It was getting late now, and I was feeling pretty lonely, stupid and angry. I was sipping my cider and had decided once it's finished I was going home. I noticed a young man starting to walk towards me. I, of course, dismiss this and imagine he'd seen a gap at the bar to order a drink, but no, he came straight over to me and started talking. He was about the same height as me. Brown curly hair which was just resting on his shoulders. He had a beard and brown eyes. He was attractive but looked like he was about 15!

"Hey, I've not seen you here before."

"Err, no, it's my first time at the Rocksoc." I weakly pull one of those smiles where your lips disappear.

"I'm in charge of the Rocksoc for the uni," he proudly announced.

"Oh right, so what does that actually mean?" I quizzed. I was actually interested in the answer.

"It means I run the night and make sure that the nights are well-attended as we get a cut of the bar and the door and then we can book artists to come to the uni."

"Oh right, that's cool. I've seen loads of bands here actually. I'm kind of impressed."

"Who have you seen this term?" he enquired.

"Well, I saw Pop Will Eat Itself, CUD, Sensor and a few others. Yes, young man, I am a gig aficionado and have the tee shirts to prove it."

"Woah! That's a great list, by the way, I'm Tim," he said with a huge smile.

I think I just passed some sort of a test? We talked and talked and then it dawned on me, he was merely enquiring to see if I could bring more people to the Rocksoc. He was trying to drum up trade. Well, I felt like a real buffoon now. Why would he have come over unless he was trying to make sure he got a cut of my drink's money from the bar? It's funny how we react to situations. I could've continued the chat; it was pleasant enough, or I could've closed the conversation down politely and moved on. Could've, would've, should've! That's not me. I'm easily offended, which turns to anger and hostility. A perfect reaction to ensure you don't keep friends, boyfriends or colleagues in the short term. My demeanour must have changed as I could see Tim's face began to gurn.

"Hey, have I said something to offend you?" he quizzed.

"No Tim, you haven't – but I think you've made your point now. You want me to bring more people from my uni to help build your bank account," I said sarcastically.

"Oh right," he responded in what looked like real shock.

"Tim – it's OK. You can go work the room somewhere else. I'm on message," I snarled.

Oh, there she is. The snarly, sarcastic and hostile version of me. Once that bitch is out – she's not put away quickly. In fact, 'handle with extreme caution' should be written on my tee-shirt right now.

"Hey, I didn't come over to drum up trade, you know, but I just figured it was a way I could come over and talk to you."

He was looking at the ground and looking very sheepish. Maybe I'd read this situation wrong? I mused.

"Oh, OK. Why?"

"Why what?"

"Why did you want to come over to talk to me?" Not to be coy, but because I was genuinely intrigued.

"Because you're pretty and I hadn't seen you here before. You'd also been standing on your own for quite some time, and I figured your friends had stood you up."

I could feel my face changing into a smile.

"You think I'm pretty?"

"Well…yeah…obviously, you're pretty."

With that, I leaned in and began to kiss him. Yes, young man – claim your prize. You found the magic words and all the night's treasures are yours! We continued to talk and make out until the lights came on. Annoyingly he had to hang around at the end of the night to make sure everyone left safely and wait for the bar to be closed and the takings to be counted. He then signed for his share which the union's manager would bank for him.

"Where do you live?" he enquired.

"At the top of Cott road."

"How are you getting home?"

"You'll walk me home, right?" I asked with a glint in my eye and raising my eyebrow at him. The universal language of 'come back to mine'.

"Oh, right – I can't actually. I'm a Halls Manager, and I have to be back into halls by 3 to do a check at the weekend. We get stupid first years leaving candles on and burning the place down if I don't do the checks." He looked as perplexed as I now felt.

"I could come around tomorrow night, and we could watch a film together?" he quickly added.

"That would be really nice."

I gave him my address, and we agreed to a 7.00 pm kick-off. He suggested he had a film we could watch, and we decide we would get a takeaway. A date. How very civilised. I made my way home lofty in the sense of romance and what might be…

The Lion King Is Rubbish

It gets to 6.30 pm, and I'd done a great job of letting all of my eight housemates know that I was having the communal living room that night as it was the only place we had a video player. I went through my prepping ritual – shower, hair, makeup and outfit. My inner voice kindly reminded me that last night he'd had beer, the lights were low, and I probably looked OK through beer goggles. What about now? What if I open the door and I can see on his face the sheer disappointment? My inner voice is such a bitch. She knows every insecurity I have and knows which cards to play at just the right moments. Too late now, the doorbell sounded. One of my housemates was quick to answer the door. He's called Amish, and he's an odd little chap. Pleasant enough but just bizarre. Can't put my finger on why. He smiles all the time – which I feel is just unnatural quite frankly. Anyway, he answered the door and shouted for me.

"Tom's here," he shouts which makes me giggle. I hear Tim correct him.

I walk out into our vast hallway – grinning.

"Hi, Tom," I said with a huge smile. Tim looked up and was smiling too. What a fabulous ice breaker.

"Did you get home OK?" he asked politely.

"Yeah, no problem."

I motioned him to the living room. I noted his hair tied back, which was kind of cute. He looked older tonight. He could pass for 18, I giggled.

"Wow, it's a massive house, Nats."

Oh, OK. He'd given me a nickname. *Not sure about that – but we'll let it float for a while before I decide if I like it,* I thought.

"Yeah, there's 9 of us who live here."

"Blimey – that is a lot. I have half a floor to manage which is 20 students. I get free digs by being a Hall's Master, so in your final year, it's good not to have to worry about being on-site or racking up more debt."

"Oh, right. You in your final year, are you?"

"Yeah, I'm doing my masters, and it's a yearlong course. I'd already incurred the debt of doing a 4-year Law degree and so wanted to do this as cheap as I could."

A couple of things struck me now:

1.   He must be at least 21 years old

2.   He was boasting again (last night about being in charge of the Rocsoc and now about reading Law and doing his Masters)

I can't describe why, but at that moment I just plainly went off him. Something in my mind just found him unattractive and annoying. *It's going to be an awkward night ahead,* I thought. He proudly presented the film.

"Have you seen The Lion King?" He proudly produced a VHS cassette tape.

"Nope. Is that the Disney cartoon thing?" I enquired. *If it is then this evening is about to get worse.*

"Yes. My mate hooked me up with a pirate copy. It's only just come out on video, but my mate managed to get me this."

He seemed really very proud of this and so with a forced smile I took it from him and popped it into the video player. We settle onto the couch and he sat right next to me and took my hand. Now, this would be a perfect date if I hadn't now decided that I find him both unattractive and annoying. We sat close to each other and I got a really strong smell of something not nice. It was his breath, it was acrid. *What the hell is going on in there,* I wonder. *Please stop breathing, Tim,* I thought. *Your breath is now making me feel a bit queasy.*

I decided I could avoid the stench if I jumped up and organised drinks. When I returned, I sat a whole seat pad away from Tim. For a few minutes, I was in a safety zone; however, Tim realised and shuffled over towards me. He then put his head on my shoulder and snuggled in – like we're a couple. This irked me even more. *Read the situation, Tim!* I thought.

The video quality was poor. It was like someone with an eighties video camera had sat on the back row of the cinema and with an unsteady hand filmed the screen. After 20 minutes of torture, I couldn't take it anymore.

"Tim, I'm struggling to watch this. The quality of the picture is making it hard to watch."

"Yeah, I agree. Let's just turn it off and do something else."

Now how to get rid of him? I got up and did some yawning and stretching.

"Are you tired?" he asked.

"Yeah, I am, actually. It was late for me last night, and I've had a full day today working at the video store."

"Yeah, I'm pretty tired too. The stupid freshers were running around till six this morning. I had to go out and have several words with them. Then I've been in the computer lab working on my thesis."

There he goes again boasting. It's time for you to jog on, mate. So we both walked and talked toward the door. At the entrance, Tim came in to kiss me. I obliged. Seemed like the fastest way to get rid of him. His kiss tasted as vile as his breath smelt. As soon as the door closed, I rush to the downstairs bathroom to brush my teeth. I was strangely satisfied with the evening. A short amount of romance and an even shorter amount of wasted time. Yes – that was entirely satisfactory. I could now watch some TV in the main living room on my own! Score!

The Best Night of My Life

Somehow, it'd got to the weekend again. It'd been a funny kind of week. I'd seen Tim twice on his campus. Not on purpose! I had had to take the decision to avoid the walk home through the neighbouring campus as I simply did not need that level of awkwardness. I caught up with my friend Page who told me her boyfriend was coming over at the weekend and the 'Wednesday night crew' were going to try a new club. Caesars Palace. It was trying a rock/metal night on Saturday, and they were having bands play downstairs. Apparently, her boyfriend liked the band that was playing, and he was coming over from Newcastle. This was the first time I'd learned that Page had a boyfriend. I'd been going out every Wednesday night with this girl for a year and never knew she had a boyfriend. How was this even possible? I was not very good at asking questions or listening to answers – so I assumed it was me. *She's probably told me, and I've forgotten,* I lament.

The week took a turn for the worse when I bumped into one of my old housemates Ian, from K-Town. He updated me on Sam and how he'd become hot property. Since 'the love of his life' dumped him, he'd been in high demand. Apparently, they'd sat and had a few drinks together while Sam appraised him of how much 'tail' he was now getting. Ian thought this was hilarious as he never really liked him, so I was kind of hurt that he'd taken the time to actually sit down with him in a pub and have more than a casual chat. Of course, I laughed along with him and feigned non-interest, but in truth I was dying on the inside. I'd spent the entire week crying myself to sleep so by the time Saturday night came around I was not in the mood to go out.

Page was very insistent, firm even. We were organised as if we were on a military manoeuvre. I guess she wanted to make sure her boyfriend's visit was a success. He was not what I was expecting. He was short, about 5 foot 6. He was super skinny. He wore the tightest black jeans you ever saw like they were spray-painted on and tucked into cowboy boots. He had backcombed long hair and lashings of black kohl eye pencil. All this I expected, but he wore a bright scarf around his head and sported big goofy glasses. Now I'll give him full marks for committing to the style. He was definitely a glam rocker. But you know how some people think they look like a million dollars and swagger – when in your own humble opinion, you think they look more like a 10 pence bargain from Woolies? Anyway, he seemed dead nice. He worked in a factory and was immensely proud of Page. I kind of felt sorry for him, as he was blissfully unaware that his beloved was lusting after dancing Dan every Wednesday night.

We got to the club, and there was a certain amount of relief that it was semi-busy. I was just not in the mood. I headed to the bar and started on Tequila. I just wanted to blot this week out. I'm not proud to say I just wanted to be as numb as soon as I could. I'm not and have never been a big drinker as I'm not a fan of the taste of alcohol or spending money. I'd make an exception tonight. By the time 10.30 pm rolled around I was not in a good way. I was definitely feeling numb – well, my face was. When I get drunk too quickly my teeth go numb. It's a strange occurrence, and it makes me laugh. I spent the next 20 minutes telling people how numb my teeth were and hitting them hard with my fingernails to prove it. Somehow it got to 12.30 am. I stood slightly swaying, alone. I then spied a tall, handsome man. He was also on his own. He was about 6 foot 4. Long, curly blond hair. He had a ridiculously beautiful face. Not my type of handsome, he was much more commercially handsome. Chiselled jaw, high cheekbones and creamy skin. Lucky for me he saw me looking at him and smiled. I smiled back. Full teeth smile – my pulling move. He wandered over to me. I'm not really sure what happened next as it's only ever happened once, but from somewhere I mustered up Moxy.

"Hey."

"Hey," I said back.

"What's so funny?" he asked.

"You are. You have no idea what I'm going to do to you tonight."

"Oh yeah? Shall we go then?" he gestured towards the exit.

"Let's."

We got into a taxi, and I gave the driver my address.

"I'm Matt."

"I don't care," I responded with a devilish grin.

"OK, I like that. I'm only visiting Hull for a night. I'm at Uni in Sheffield, studying architecture."

In truth I'm surprised I can remember any of this ;) We got to my house, and I paid the taxi. I got my keys out and

142

Matt got them into the lock and opened my door. Thankfully, my bedroom was first on the right. We entered and I launched myself onto him. Even though I was entirely drunk, I was still self-aware. Still trying to figure out the lighting potential so my round tummy was not on show.

We were now snogging hard, deep, ferociously. There's electricity emanating from both of us. Sparks flying, bouncing off every surface. His kiss was hot and passionate. His tongue searching my mouth and his hands holding the back of my head tight. Inevitably, we were now rapidly getting undressed. I jumped under my faithful candlewick bedspread and was panting. I was so ready for what's about to happen. He's on top of me, and now I could sense how tall he was. His head was at the same height as mine but his body and legs seemed to go on and on. Using his legs, he pinned my legs down and completed a straddle manoeuvre. His weight on me was a sensation I've not had before. It's exciting and welcomed. The connection between us was intense. There was moaning and panting and desire, and it's charged. He was masterful and found all the right positions to make me submit to him. This was wild, frantic and every part of my body was excited. He moved around me with ease. *Wow, this is the first man to have really given me pleasure.* I purred. I'd never felt so turned on before – ever. I was pretty sure we both climaxed, and when we had, we laid with the tingling of amazing sex just ringing around our bodies. We lay just looking at each other. Our eyes were locked, and there was a sense of togetherness as we fell asleep. In the morning, Matt stirred and started to get up.

"Hey," he whispered.

"Hey," I smiled back.

"Thanks for last night, I really needed it." Somehow his eyes looked sad this morning.

"I'm here in Hull visiting my friend Sophie. She's helping me get over my ex."

"Oh, and did Sophie manage to help you get over your ex?" I was a little puzzled at his comment.

"Yeah. Sophie is my best friend from school. I reckon I'll be in trouble when I rock up this morning as I didn't even say goodbye to her last night."

"Yeah, well, things moved quite quickly," I said with a smile emerging.

"They did, indeed," he smiled broadly back at me.

We knew this had been a one-off and what a one-off it was. The afterglow had me smiling all day. In the early evening, I was travelling back to K-town and had packed my bag quickly, having left it until the last minute. I'd slept most of the day but had had to get a wriggle on to get to the coach station. I turned up and got in the National Express queue. I hated the coach, but it was £15, and the train was £100 so if I wanted to nip home, it was the only way to possibly afford it. I was grabbing a few days at home as I was still smarting over the news of Sam and I just wanted to be around my family. Sometimes you just need to be at home, right?

As I waited and the queue shortened, I was still heady with the thrill of the night before. I got to my seat and arranged my bag under it. I got my Walkman out and began to look out over the coach station. It's pretty ugly, and there were a lot of sorry-looking people roaming the station. From the corner of my eye, I spotted a girl that I saw from the previous night. I recognised her as she was staring hard at me when I was talking with Matt. In the next moment, I saw Matt. *Holy hell.*

He's getting on the coach. No god, why? Please don't be getting on this bus. I don't want that awkwardness. Last night was a one-off. A special. I could see him begin to climb the stairs. *OK, maybe he'll take a seat at the front, and we won't have that awkwardness. Oh, dear god, he's seen me!* I half-smile and half grimace. He saw me but didn't see me. He was just as beautiful as I remembered from this morning. He walked past me and sat several rows behind me. Of course! The coach called in at Sheffield. He's going back to Sheffield. Thankfully, I must have fallen asleep as when I awoke, we'd already dropped off at Sheffield. I was kind of glad, but I was also kind of sad. He clearly only wanted it to be one-night, and that's OK – but gosh, that was one fantastic night!

Too Much Already

After being home for a week – it was too much already. Once you'd tasted the freedom of living without your parents, going back to the nest is just too hard. My rents were getting on my nerves. I'd secured a job back in the factory, but this time I was on the sewing machines. The flatbed machine to be accurate. This time I was stitching make up bags together for Boots and Marks and Spencers. They were really chintzy. Probably destined for the post-Christmas sale table, I mused. It was piece rate so for the shift 8–4.30, I had my head down and tried to make the most out of the crappy job. I didn't mind it too much as the radio was on and each song was another 3 minutes closer to being done. Friday after work, I headed straight for the coach station. I was travelling back to Hull. I needed some time to process the semester. Its ups and downs, and I needed the familiarity of my bedroom at uni. My parents had given my bedroom up to my brother Alan. He'd been dishonourably discharged on drugs charges from the Army. To be fair to Alan, he'd never have touched drugs. He was and is anti-drugs – but his friends were not. He'd got caught up with a wrong group, and they had stashed drugs in everyone's rooms. Anyone with drugs in their room was discharged. My mum and dad had moved when Alan left for the army and downsized. No one expected him back. So, there was no room for him. Well, except my room. So when I returned home, I was given a put up bed in conservatory with no wardrobe space or drawers. It was a complete piss-take.

So, I decided I'd go back to Hull for the weekends where at least I had a bedroom. My friends Page, Paula, Glenn and Phil were still knocking about Hull so we agreed to go out for a night out at Spiders. I'd received approval to stop working the summer shifts, and so it was nice to not be behind the cast iron web, where I was usually imprisoned. As we queued up outside, we chatted. We'd not been out together for ages, and we were all up for a good laugh. Page and Paula lived together. Paula's dad had bought an actual house in Hull and was covering the mortgage with renting students. I was always a little jealous that I was never offered the opportunity to rent a room with them. However, Page and Paula could be a bit wet – so it may have been a lucky escape. As we entered, I noticed a new face behind the pay desk. I sensed a little niggle in my gut – a little jealous feeling.

"Don't get comfortable," I said to her and shot her a smile.

She probably wondered who the hell I was but Ray, the lead bouncer, heard me and smiled.

"Don't you worry, Natasha, she's a bench warmer."

He gave me a nod and a wink. He was a nice old boy, Ray. He was a menacing size with a face that had seen a lot of punches over the years, but he was a lovely bloke. He would run and fetch me water during my shifts, as it got seriously hot in that little cubby hole and for that I owed him. The night was a bit of a bust. With all the students returning home for the summer holidays, the club was pretty quiet. The students who lived in Hull and were returning to Hull for their summer holidays were indeed new faces, but there just weren't that many of them. Phil knew one of them, some lad called Chris. They'd shared a lift to a gig one time, and so the two of them chatted. He was only about 5' 6 tall. He had reddish-brown hair and was afflicted with a sombre looking face. I talked to him for a little while, but he was hard work. His friends eventually showed up and one of them caught my eye. A tall, willowy young man. Short brown hair. Dressed in really ordinary clothes. Blue jeans, blue tee-shirt and trainers. He'd made zero effort. I'll never know why it's OK for men to make no effort. Is it because they think they don't have to? Is it because they are trying to look like they've purposefully made no effort as a style statement? So annoying – but when the available options are limited, it will do.

"Hi, you're Phil's friend, right?" I casually enquired.

He turned to face me, and his face told me I was not his type. He looked me up and down and pulled a slightly contorted mouth.

"Yeah. Sorry, who are you?" he asked with disdain.

"I'm Natasha. I'm a friend of Phil," I responded, matching his disdain. Yes, sunny Jim, you're not my type either!

"Oh yeah, he's a good guy. We shared a ride to Metallica in Sheffield a couple of months ago."

"Yeah, I know. That's the only reason I'm saying hello," I couldn't load my response with any more acidity.

Sensing my attitude, he softened his face.

"Hey, sorry if I was a bit off a minute ago. I've had a totally shit day, and I'm in a bit of a grump, to be honest." He gave me a small smile.

"Yeah I've had a pretty shitty week, to be fair," I shot him a part smile.

"Let's get a drink and compare stories," he suggested.

"Great idea," I smiled, properly this time.

So we chatted through our horror stories of how we'd both had to work and do shitty jobs and described just how shitty those jobs were. We talked about uni. He was at Leeds Uni, and so I quizzed him all about the campus, the nightlife, the course and whatever it took to keep him chatting. What the past 12 months of rubbish relationships and one-night stands had taught me was that there was a direct correlation between the length of time you keep a prospect chatting to the likelihood of getting off with them. So naturally, we ended back at his. I wish I could tell you more, but mainly it was so below average I can't remember the details – just his name. If the sex is so average – does it even count, I wonder.

And a Few More Notches

It was Sunday night, and Andy (the housemate) knocked on my bedroom door.

"Your dad's on the phone, Nat."

These are the words you never want to hear when you have a dad who never calls. He's not good at staying in touch, that's my mother's job. So as soon as I heard he was on the phone, I knew something is wrong.

"Nat, it's your dad. I've got some news."

"Dad, what's going on?" I asked.

"Your mum's had confirmed today that she's got secondary cancer. It's nothing to worry about yet, and it's treatable."

As an ex-soldier, my dad has a way of delivering news in a very matter-of-fact way. I heard the words, but my head had fogged up. I felt like my mind was drowning, and I could hear the sea in my ears.

"What does she have, Dad?" I asked.

The first time she got cancer, she had Non-Hodgkin's Lymphoma. The advice was that she was terminal. I was 13. The parents told me as little as possible, and it was by accident that I overheard a conversation with the oncologist one evening, which alerted me to the knowledge that she would soon die. I was unable to address my fear and feelings at the time as I knew that to be helpful to my parents, I needed them not to worry about me, so continued to be the role model child.

We ended up having to sell our home. It was a large six-floor Victorian house. We'd lived there for seven years, and it was the first time I'd experienced stability and roots. So now I had to combat losing my home, my friends and to keep it all still together. It was a ridiculously tough time. In what was a miracle, my mother got better. She endured chemo, radiotherapy and against all the odds, the brave, resilient woman pulled through.

"What's the prognosis, Dad, the real prognosis?"

"We don't know, Nat, and that's the truth."

"Can I speak to Mum?"

"Not right now, Nat, she's a bit upset and wants some time to process, but she'll come 'round," he said.

I came off the phone and put my shoes and coat on and walked. That week was a blur. There was Ben, Chris, Pete, Spencer and Paul. That much I have written down. I don't remember much else. EUPD at its finest. Thank you, next!

The Next Mistake

In general, all my encounters have been mini rehearsals, and so I wouldn't say that any were mistakes – until now. This was not my finest moment. I was back home. I had decided to stay in K-town for the weekend as Lizzie had assured me I could stay at hers. So, after her Saturday shift at the dry cleaners, we headed back to hers. We chit chatted as usual. She doesn't wear make-up, and so she continued to drink through my getting ready ritual. Eventually, we got around to me creating an opportunity to casually enquire after Sam whilst pretending to not be interested in the answer – but I casually asked,

"So have you seen Sam around?"

There was a noticeable pause, and she looked up at me.

"Nat, you don't still like him, do you?"

There's something in the way she asked me that told me she was about to give me some hard to swallow news. My stomach tightened, and I was trying really hard to look disinterested and casual all at the same time.

"God, no, he's a prick." I spitted.

I could feel my throat drying, and I was feeling the prickle of hot tears. *Hold it together*, I repeated in my head like a meditative chorus.

"Oh good, coz I was wondering how I'd tell you this, but I got off with him last week, and, well, we shagged."

Her face was pensive.

"Oh my god, why would you want to do that?" I said, forcing a laugh.

My internal voice was quizzing me hard. *Is this how I should react? Is this how a person who is not bothered would respond? Am I convincing her? Does she buy it?*

"We just got talking and drinking and ended up back here."

I could feel my chest tightening, and my breathing was struggling a bit now. I couldn't tell if I was upset, angry, jealous or what. All I knew was that I was not OK. Somehow, we managed to change the subject and make our way out. We chatted and had a laugh, but my mind kept roaming back to that moment where she spoke the words 'well, we shagged'. It was painful to replay yet my mind was going to replay this all night long. The night went very, very slowly. *How could she do this to me?* I wondered.

We queued up for the night bus. I just wanted to be at home now. My home in Hull. I now hated K-town and everyone in it. Sensing my mood, Lizzie decided to sit with some random blokes and I was relieved. I sat on the seats at the back of the bus and stared out of the window. I was really good at taking a situation and using my inner voice to make the situation a hundred times worse, working myself into a stupor. The bus pulled into Bingley, and more people boarded the bus. Some random bloke made his way to the back of the bus and sat next to me. He chuntered to the bloke sat next to him. I zoned them out. The next thing I knew his hand was on my knee. He was tapping it, trying to get my attention.

"Oh, right, do you want me?"

"Yes, are you OK?" he asked.

"Yes, why?"

"You look really sad is all?"

"Oh, yeah, a bit. Just had some bad news and I'm a bit down about it."

"Do you want a hug?" he asked.

"Yeah, I do, actually."

So he leaned over and started to hug me. I did feel better. He was tallish with long reddish blond hair. He was not handsome, nor was he bad looking. Just average.

"I'm Steve," he said.

"Hey, Steve."

"I don't think you should be on your own tonight," he said with concern.

"I'm not on my own. I'm with my mate, Lizzie, and with that," I pointed towards her.

"Oh, you're friends with Liz. She's a good laugh," he said energetically.

"Oh, you shagged her too?" I added while rolling my eyes.

"What? No. Definitely not. I know her brother is all."

"Ah, right. I've not met him."

"Yeah, we went to school together," he added.

"OK," I said curtly. I was really not in the mood. I wanted to be left to feel my sorrow. To dwell in my self-pity but Steve was not having it and persevered. By the time we got to K-town, he had worked hard to get me to talk. Lizzie came to the back of the bus and noticed I was sat with Steve.

"You're reet," she said in her usual broad Yorkshire accent.

"Reet," Steve said in response.

"Nat, are we gonna walk up to mine or are we getting a taxi?"

Steve wrapped his arm around my shoulder and said, "She's staying at mine tonight."

I was surprised at this, but my face didn't show it. Instead, I looked at Lizzie and give her a wink. I was trying desperately hard not to show her just how sad I was and how her words had broken my heart and me.

"Oh, you sure, Nat?"

I think it was concern in her eyes. But I was not able to take her interest seriously. Where was her concern for me when she slept with the greatest love of my life? Where was the consideration of my feelings then? No, this would be much better. I wouldn't have to look at her scabby, ugly, miserable face a moment longer. Ah – there it was. Anger. It had taken several hours to show up, but it was coursing through me now like I was supercharged.

"So, where do you live, Steve?"

"Just on Hainsworth Road."

That was a 2-minute walk from the bus station. *That is absolutely great. I can be asleep in the next 20 minutes,* I thought. I looked at Steve and smiled. He took this as permission to lean in for a kiss. I obliged. I was not really processing any feelings at this time and had chosen an armour of numbness. I was merely going through the motions. We arrived at his house, and he invited me to sit on the sofa. I obliged. We started to kiss again, and within 5 minutes it was over. The deed had been done. At last, I could sleep.

I was up early the next day and let myself out. I was feeling icky, no shame. It was consensual, and Steve wasn't pushy or anything, but I knew it was a mistake. However, I was going to forgive myself as who makes good decisions when they are at their lowest? Still hurting, I made it back to my parents' house. Avoiding the questions on the night out, I went back to my makeshift room and slept.

My mother was looking unwell. Her eyes were sunken and she'd lost so much weight that she looked frail. She and my dad had done their best to put a brave face on things but I could hear how worried they were.

"Nat, I really don't want you to worry. I'll kick cancer's butt again. Just like I did before," she said being resolute.

"The only worry I want you to have is making sure you get the best degree you can get."

"So what have the consultants told you? What's the treatment plan?"

"Well, I've had a liver biopsy and they think they can remove part of it that's cancerous and then use chemo to blast the rest of it. It's not actually as drastic as my first cancer. So they are really hopeful of a good recovery."

The words were aimed at providing me hope but instead I heard 'hopeful of a good recovery'. Not a full recovery. I could sense that she hadn't got all the facts about the procedure and process yet and so to keep asking her questions felt like it would simply antagonise her and I didn't want to be responsible for that. So I resigned myself to 'playing along' and spurting platitudes:

'You'll do great, Mum, you're such a fighter.'

'Cancer won't know what's hit it, you don't mess with my mum.'

She cordially laughed and we both knew we were both play acting, but it was enough for now.

Yorkie

Still languishing back in my hometown I began feeling the mental strain. I didn't want to be here, but I didn't want to be in Hull either. I was positively without a place to call home. Everything and everyone was annoying the crap out of me. I was beyond irritable. I didn't know why! OK, truth time. I did know why. I was angry. Pissed. How does a so-called friend sleep with my ex? I searched my feelings and they were still there. Buried very, very deep. Loss. Rejection. The sense of despair, abandonment. A whole heap of feelings I numbed after our breakup. I didn't deal with any of them, and the revelation that Lizzie casually slept with him was so hurtful. Beyond words. I felt so betrayed.

#girlcode you do not sleep with someone's ex unless you get approval before the said act. I'm not even sure that that is what was eating me up either. My studies were not going well, I was struggling to focus. I was so easily distracted. I was apprehensive about the next semester as I needed to pull an ace out of the bag in my finals and score firsts across the board in my finals if I was to end up with a 2:1. I couldn't keep coasting as I had been. *So maybe I should quit?* I wondered. I knew I was not being serious and just trying to provoke a new inner dialogue to stop me thinking about Sam and 'her'.

WTAF! The additional pressure of Mum not being well and her words ringing around my head, like a threat. 'Make sure you do the best you can at university'. I hadn't given my best in months.

As the weekend was rolling around again, my mood had not changed. I was avoiding Lizzie, and that was making me anxious too. I couldn't bear the thought of staying in on Saturday night and watching Pop Idol or whatever crappy TV was on. But I couldn't go out with Lizzie. I was just too angry, so I called Sarah. She had been off the radar recently as she'd met someone new. I was pleased for her and everything, but as all new relationships blossomed old ones lay fallow. I'd missed her, a lot. After much begging, I managed to get her to agree to come out with me. The proviso that her new beau would come out too. So the 3 of us met in the village centre to queue up for the loser cruiser into K-town. The bus ride usually was fun, but tonight it was less so. Watching Sarah and Paul snuggle, kiss and share in-jokes was enough to make any romantic say 'enough already'. I sat on my own and stared out of the window, it was a 40-minute bus journey, and that's a long time to sit and stare.

My inner voice working overtime:

1. I'll be alone forever
2. I'm such a loser – no, a big fat failure at everything
3. How the hell will I be able to get firsts in all my exams?
4. No one will ever fancy me
5. I want to go back to Hull
6. I miss my uni friends
7. What will I do if I see Sam?

These themes just whirled around in my head on repeat, so I was pretty keyed up by the time we got to the pub. I was now determined to have the best night ever (this is the phrase I use when I subconsciously know my aim is to get so drunk I don't have to deal with anything anymore). A need to drown out my inner monologue so she can't be heard anymore. Numbness visits.

I was eager to see if Luke would turn up. I could do with some fruitless flirting and exciting conversation. Finally, I caught a break, Luke appeared. We hadn't seen each other in a year or so. His face hadn't changed one bit. His friend Kevin saw me and nodded at me, a polite hello. I bee-lined to Luke and began to make a big fuss about how we hadn't seen each other in ages, and he was smiling. His face had actually lit up. That's just the validation I needed. Someone was happy to see me. We talked about all sorts, never touching once on relationships. It's a forbidden topic. I didn't want to hear he had met someone and, clearly, he didn't want to know either. He smelled so good, it was intoxicating. The feeling I had was electric. My skin was very sensitive and every time I laughed, I touched his arm, which simultaneously gave me goose pimples all over. Kevin joined us eventually.

"Hey, Natasha. You OK, long time no see."

He's a nice guy, Kevin. He looks a bit like Tom Cruise in his early twenties. Very conventionally handsome. Not my type.

"Hey, Kevin. It's been ages. I'm great thanks," I gushed.

"Well, sorry to say that I need Luke as we are expected at a family party – so time to move out, Luke," he said. He gave Luke a pretty stern nod. The one that means 'we have to go'.

"Oh, OK," I said, swallowing my disappointment.

I quickly checked the clock on the wall and it read 11.30 pm. It was still early. Luke made his excuse to go to the toilet and left Kevin and me to chat.

"Natasha, are you ever going to ask Luke out? If you wait for him to ask you out, you'll be dead."

I was really taken aback. How would Kevin know I was interested in Luke?

"What are you on about, Kev, we are just friends?"

"Yeah, right. That's bullshit, and you know it. Just ask him out already."

Two thoughts went through my head. I either continue to deny my feelings for him, or I enquire if he thought Luke might be interested. Fuelled by a lot of alcohol, I decided to be bold. Take a chance.

"If I asked him out, would he say yes, though?"

"I really have no idea. Luke never talks about you or anything, but clearly, you like him, so ask him out."

This cut me deep. In all the years we'd been 'talking and flirting', neither Kevin nor Luke had ever raised the possibility of Luke and me getting together – NEVER!!! There had been no discussion between mates about 'that Natasha'. All of those pre-existing self-doubts flooded my mind. They had never ever ever discussed me, how could that be? For one solitary second, I surmised he was lying and then added – *why would he? He has nothing to gain or lose.* I was now spiralling. My thoughts were muddled, and I was devastated. My stomach was knotted, and it felt like I was being wound up like a set of cogs getting tighter and tighter. Luke reappeared and smiled at me. I weakly smiled back. As he began to put his coat on, Kevin put his hand on my arm. He leaned in and spoke quietly,

"Natasha, Luke never talks about any girl. He's so shy, but I think he really likes you. You should ask him out."

He'd clearly noticed my change of mood and could probably see the tears prickling behind my eyes. I was now wondering if he'd just being kind to me to make me feel less rotten. I bid them goodbye and found myself at the bar. Yes, I was just going to get drunk. It was nearing 2 pm, and I was rat-arsed. I was leaning against a wall and wondering if Sarah and Paul (her new beau) would help peel me off the wall and get me into a taxi. I was also not bothered if they didn't. I could easily lay on the pavement and sleep. I didn't really feel like I cared about anything right now.

"Hey, you live in Silsden, don't you?" I heard a voice from behind me. I turned slowly to see who it was that was making the noise.

"Shhh. You're too loud, sir," I slurred.

He laughed and leaned into me.

"OK, I'm whispering now. Do you want to share a taxi back to Silsden?"

I recognised him as he got the morning bus with me. He's the same height as me but a few years older. He had dirty blond curly hair – but something was different about him.

"You've cut your hair, sir."

I smiled, in fact, I was grinning. I was now aware that I could feel a numbness in my mouth. I couldn't feel my teeth. I knew this was a sign that I was bona fide pissed. I started to tap them with my nails.

"My teeth are numb," I giggled.

"I think you need someone to take you home safely," he said.

I nodded. We walked to the taxi rank, and I was lolloping on him.

"Who are you?"

"My mates call me Yorkie."

Yorkie. What kind of name is that, I wondered, but I was nonplussed either way. Going home to bed sounded like a plan. We got into the taxi and he asked where I lived. I told the taxi driver and insisted I'm dropped off first.

"Is there someone at home who can look after you?"

"Nope." I hiccupped.

"No," he repeated.

"Well, come to mine so I can keep an eye on you."

There was something safe about him. I don't know what it was, but my gut was saying I could trust him. So I nodded. He kept talking to me on the way to his place. He lived on the totally opposite side of the village from me.

"Do you live alone?" I asked.

"No, I still live with my parents, but they are on holiday with my twin brother."

"You have a twin?"

"Yes, we are identical except he's got long hair."

"Oh, he's the fit one," I blurted out.

"What?" Yorkie laughed.

"He gets on my morning bus, I fancy him."

"Oh, do you now?"

He was rolling his eyes at me. I now felt bad. They were actually identical and other than the length of hair there wasn't really anything to decide between.

"Well, yeah, cos I like men with long hair, but you're fit too," I added for good measure.

He was laughing hard now.

"You are soooooo drunk, young lady," he stated but gave me a smile that said he kind of liked it – my sass that is.

"I'm drunk, I know, but I can still recognise a fit bloke when I see one," and I shot him 'the smile'. I was not sure one bit of what I was saying or what I was doing. I guess I was feeling lonely, rejected. I wanted some attention. We eventually pulled up to his house and he helped me out of the taxi.

"I'll show you to my parents' room, and you can stay there," he said.

We walked up the stairs in silence, and he opened the door to what appeared to be a master bedroom.

"Do you want some water or something?"

"Yes, please," I said rather sheepishly.

I don't want this to be it, I though. I wanted to kiss him. So when he reappeared and said 'goodnight', I launched at him. Subtle, it wasn't, but he responded. We kissed with force and passion and I started to unbutton his shirt. We reclined onto the bed and as we kissed, hands were searching and touching flesh. I can feel how excited he was and so I went straight in to relieve him from his pants. He tugged my knickers off albeit my skirt was still on. He then pushed my knees up to my chest and leaned heavy on me. *Holy fuck, this feels good.* I'd not had someone so masterfully manage my limbs before, and I liked it. It felt deep, hot and sexy. He had stamina, and I appreciated it. Giving just the right number of moans to encourage but not sound like a cheap porn star, I could sense he was close to climaxing, and I was not, but it didn't matter. I was feeling good and enjoying it. With a few more rhythmic pushes, he was spent. He was spent, and I was happy. In the morning, I woke up alone. As my eyes began to register my surroundings, I was smiling as I had a good time. I had no qualms about getting up and letting myself out. There was no need for pleasantries. I was hanging, but my good mood was helping a lot. On my way home I decided I was going to ask Luke out. Yes. Why had I been so afraid? *I'm a grown arsed woman who has just had mind-blowing sex with a stranger. That's pretty adventurous, I think. Albeit others might say totally stupid/idiotic. But for now, I'm riding the crest of the wave.*

"Hello, can I speak to Luke?"

"Who is it please?" says a man who I could only assume was Luke's dad.

"It's Natasha," I respond.

"Does he know you?" his dad asked.

"I hope so," I responded indignantly.

Just get him already, I thought to myself.

"Hello."

"Hey, Luke, it's Natasha," I said.

Holy shit. I was no longer riding the wave. I felt sick. Nerves and butterflies were moving around my stomach. I now had nothing to say.

"Hi, Natasha – how did you get my number?"

Shit! Shit! Shit! I could hardly say I looked through the phone book and through diligent detective skills and some wrong dialling, I found him.

"Does it matter?" I asked pompously trying to deflect the question.

"No, I don't suppose it does."

"Look, I wondered if you fancied going out next week with me?"

What on earth are the weird words that have just come out of my mouth?

"Oh, err, to do what?" he said.

What the actual fuck! Help me out here, Luke!

"I don't know. Anything. Just a drink at the rat?" I added nonchalantly.

"I'm actually busy next Saturday," he replied.

"Oh, OK. Never mind then."

I really had nothing else to add. If he didn't want to go out, then he'd just told me, right?

"Well, I have a family party," he added limply.

I was now simply not believing a word of it. I felt pretty annoyed and if you are not interested, then just say so, I think.

"OK, Luke. Sure – whatever. I just thought I'd ask as we seem to have been pussyfooting around for a long time now. But I get it. You're not interested. Fair enough," I said with attitude. I don't know where this moxy was coming from, but I felt like I didn't want to waste my time anymore.

"No, seriously, I have a family party. I could get to the Rat, but it would be after midnight. But I'm up for meeting if that's OK with you?"

Something in his tone had changed. He seemed like he was trying to be sincere.

"OK. Well, I'll be out so I will be in the Trap after midnight. I'll be standing in the usual corner – so just find me when you get there," I added.

"Yeah, sure. I'll see you on Saturday night," he added.

I sat and smiled. I could not believe what I had just done. But I had finally scored a date with Luke! This was a big deal, and so I called my aunt Charlotte to tell her, I needed her help. I needed an outfit, hairstyling, and make up – the lot. My aunt is a hairdresser and super cool. She's 6 years older than me and was in her early twenties then. She was very excited to hear my news and told me to come to her salon on Saturday and I could be her last appointment. She was going to give me a makeover. **Squeeeeeallllll**.

Her salon colleagues were all mid-twenties too. They were complete 'townies' and did not share my sense of style. Charlotte had brought a range of clothes for me to try on. I landed on a green wool blazer which was the colour of fresh-cut grass. It was not my style, but I liked it. She blew out my bob and it looked good. I could hardly contain the butterflies and my excitement was visible within a 10-mile radius. I was also very nervous. I'm super shy at the best of times, and now there was a new consideration. He knew. He knew I liked him. Before there existed doubt. Now there was none. He now had the upper hand as I had asked him out.

I was in the pub for 9 pm with Sarah and Paul. She was giddy with excitement.

"Finally, Nat," said Sarah followed by, "about bloody time," and she laughed.

"Sarah, what am I gonna talk about?" I asked.

"It'll just flow. Don't even worry about it. You two can talk for England once you get going so why will it be any different?"

"Yeah, maybe."

Just before the bewitching hour Sarah and I went to the toilets to refresh my make-up and so I could have one last hyper maniacal conversation about how excited yet scared I was. I'd been careful not to drink too much, but just enough I had a warm buzz – to take the edge off. We exited the loos and walked through the bustling nightlife at the Rat Trap. I could see my spot in the corner where I always stood. Comforted by the walls on either side. No one could flank me. I also had the ideal view of the stairs, so when Luke would appear at the top, I'd see him. I waited. I wasn't really aware of anything going on around me. I was in my own head. Rambling and swirling thoughts, checking my watch. Ten past midnight. *OK,* I thought. *That's OK, he could be walking into town and maybe misjudged how long it would take him.* I wasn't worried. Well, that's a slight lie. I was a little worried. Half past 12. This was not OK and yet part of me was still hoping he'd just waylaid and would be with me shortly. Finally, at 1 am, Sarah put her arm around me and said, "He's not coming, Nat. He's chickened out."

We shared a look that only best friends can share. The one where one is telling the other: It's OK. Keep it together, and we can languish in your sorrow in private. My face was communicating back, 'How soon can we leave so I can sob my eyes out?'

Sarah grabbed my hand and whispered something to Paul. She tugged at my hand, and we left. Straight to the taxi rank in silence. We loaded ourselves into the taxi, and Sarah just put her arm around me and let me gently sob. Gutted. There are no other words. I resolved that night I would NEVER EVER ask a man out again. It was simply too painful.

Tumblers or Bust

Somehow through my pain, I decided to pick up the phone to Lizzie. I needed sympathy, and she was good at that stuff. I also wanted to do something reckless and she was easy to convince to enable me. I explained about my heartbreak, and she demanded that we go out that Friday to Tumblers nightclub. Tumblers was a student club attached to Bradford University. It was frequented by artsy types and alternatives. It was a bit pretentious for my liking, but it was nowhere near K-town, and I couldn't go to Rios in Bradford anymore either. For 12 months I'd pretty much created situations that I was uncomfortable with from all my local pubs and clubs, so Tumblers would have to be OK. We met at the usual spot, outside the National Express Office in K-town. I loved this location as the office had adverts in its windows. Deals to concerts and gigs in other cities. We'd while away the time discussing which bands we'd go and see – knowing neither of us could afford it. On this particular occasion, the gig scene was quite light, so instead, we looked at the coach holidays.

"Shall we book a trip to Austria?" Lizzie asked.

My mind went immediately to Mans. "No, I don't want any type of Scandi adventure, thank you very much," I chortled.

"What are you laughing at?"

"Wait until we get on the bus and I'll tell you," I said with an eye roll.

"Ace! A Nat story," she responded. She knew me too well.

Our bus trip was reasonably unadventurous, and we had set off before having a drink, so we were both pretty low key. We'd discussed where to go for a drink once we were in Bradford, but in truth, it was pretty poor, so reluctantly we decided to go straight to Tumblers. That way we'd get access to the cheap entrance fee, so there was some justification. I was really not familiar with its layout and so appreciated a bit of time to understand it and the bar situation. There was literally no one else there. We ordered a couple of pints of cider and black and went to an area with tables. We chatted over the previous weeks' adventures with 'Steven'. Not my greatest moment but I didn't want to get into it with Lizzie. Lizzie was relaying to me just how lonely she'd become since we all left K-town and how she was looking for a special someone. It wasn't a conversation we'd ever really had. It was a reality I wasn't used to. Lizzie being vulnerable. Somehow, I felt comforted that she was hurting. Not heartbreak pain – just general numbness to what was a pretty bleak existence. She'd taken a job in the local dry cleaners and while I think she enjoyed her days, meeting people and socialising – her evenings were empty. I realised we were even more alike than I'd known or understood. We took pleasure from each other's company as we essentially created chaos when together. We needed the distraction, and so we agreed that 'that night' was going to be the stuff of legends. The advantage of being first in is essentially you get to see the male buffet. As each male

169

walked past, we gave each other knowing glances. Essentially rating them as they paraded past. Occasionally we'd either 'phwoaaaaaaar' or 'errrrrrr no' at each other. We were now merrily past our second pint and dancing was on the cards. A bit of Pulp and 'modern people'. We were up our arms flailing all about and singing along at the top of our voices. We surreptitiously checked out the males dancing on the dancefloor. I became aware of a nauseating feeling in the bottom of my stomach. I noticed a man in my periphery vision who resembled Sam. I stopped dancing and could feel a wave of angst roll over me. It was a very physical reaction. Cold sweat, tightening knots in the pit of my stomach and nausea. The man was coming towards me.

"Hi, Nat."

I stood motionless. Fight, flight or freeze. You guessed it – frozen to the spot.

Lizzie bopped over.

"Hi, Sam, what are you doing here?"

"I'm here with Ellen. We are kind of hanging out."

With the blood returning to my face I found my voice.

"Hi, Sam, long-time no see."

He turned and smiled at me. A smile as if we were good friends. This was totally new territory for me, and I didn't like it. I didn't want to be there anymore. I had to get away, and so I motioned to Lizzie that I was going to the loo. She nodded. I sat on the loo. Still frozen, pure brain fog. I didn't want to address how I felt as I knew that if I gave it airtime, I'd be in pieces. The hurt and pain were too much for me to bear and I just sat trying to push it all down. Every moment it bubbled away in my stomach, I could feel myself closer to tears. It had been 14 months since we split and yet I still hadn't grieved. I refused to. So facing this amount of rejection and pain I knew my reaction. I would get blind drunk and create seismic chaos and 'show' him just how over him I was.

I went to the bar and returned to Lizzie with shots in my hands.

"Down the hatch, girl!" I said as I shoved two shots into her hands.

"What are they?"

"Does it matter?" I said with a wicked smile.

"Haha, suppose not!"

And with that, we drank the shots. One straight after the other.

"Your round."

Twenty minutes later, I could feel the warm buzz of an alcoholic haze crawling over my skin and I could sense my teeth feeling numb. The sign that things were about to get out of hand and messy. Just the drama I needed. Lizzie and I danced over to the dance floor and began to throw shapes, and when I say shapes, I have literally no idea what we danced to or how we danced, but we went for it. The numbness I felt was welcome. I felt fuzzy and uninhibited, and the night felt like a stretch of endless possibilities.

At some point I realised I'd lost Lizzie. Where was she? I didn't have my glasses on, and I could only see a couple of metres around me, and she wasn't in that space. I thought I'd better go and search for her. *Maybe she's just gone to the loo,* I wondered. I moved to the edge of the dance floor realising I couldn't remember the direction of the toilets.

"Are you looking for Lizzie?" a voice asked. It was from Sam.

"Yeah, you seen her?"

"Yeah, she's talking to that youth over there." He was pointing.

I could make out long blonde hair, and a figure stood next to it.

"OK, thanks."

I eventually could see Lizzie full in the throes of conversation. She saw me out of the corner of her eye.

"Naaaaaaat," she slurred.

"Lizzieeeeeeee," I sarcastically responded.

"Nat, this is Reuben and his friend Wesley."

"You're making that up," I said loudly and with disbelief.

"I'm not," she laughed.

"Hey," said the blond man who looked 16. His friend was small with a short crew cut. He smiled up at me and so I politely smiled back.

"I'm Wes," he said.

Now we all know how this works. Your friend fancies someone and you get lumbered keeping their friends entertained. *Well, not tonight sunshine,* I thought. *I'm not babysitting for Lizzie tonight.* I smiled at him and turned on my heel. I thought I'd just go and dance. I didn't mind dancing on my own when I was drunk. I didn't care that I was mainly the only person dancing alone. I didn't know anyone and so who cares? As I turned to face in the general direction of Lizzie I noticed that Wes had followed me onto the dance floor. I was slightly amused at this show of confidence. *OK, Wes,* I thought. *I'll dance with you.* So we danced. It was actually good fun. Then Sam appeared.

"Is that your new boyfriend?" he said mockingly.

I felt stung by his words. Irked even. I wanted to be anywhere else at that moment. As if sensing this Wesley launched at me. He was probably only 5 foot 6 and was possibly on his tiptoes as he reached up at me and kissed me. I was really taken aback but interestingly, drunk or not, it felt good. He was a really good kisser. With my eyes closed I couldn't see him on his tiptoes, so that worked. When we surfaced, Sam was nowhere to be seen. I felt immediately better.

"Wesley, what was all that about?" I asked.

"I just wanted to kiss you as I think you're fit," he said.

Eloquent it was not, but effective it was. I smiled a broad smile. Not my 'winning' smile, more of a totally amused smirk. Lizzie motioned us over and suggested we all split and go find a kebab shop. Food was a good idea. *Let's soak up the alcohol and see what the damage is,* I thought. We found an eatery and all ordered food. I think they were probably just as drunk as us. Lizzie explained that she and Reuben had agreed that we were all meeting tomorrow and going on a picnic. I thought this was hilarious.

"What are we – the Bronte sisters?" I joked.

"Seriously, Nat. Reuben is going to drive from Baildon to K-town and pick us up."

"What time is all this happening?"

"11 ish," Reuben said.

I cackled.

"I won't be out of bed till way after 2 pm – so good luck with that."

"Nat, I'll get you up."

I could sense Lizzie was not happy I wasn't playing along. We all got on the night bus home. We were near the front of the queue and so were able to get seats together. Wes sat next to me and was holding my hand. I wasn't sure how I felt about it, so I decided not to make any kind of deal with it. Sam then popped up out of the stairwell with Ellen. He clocked us and decided to come sit in the seats next to us 4. He started talking to Lizzie.

"Who's that loser?" Wes asked. This really made me chuckle.

"My ex."

"Oh really? Well, he needs to fuck right off then doesn't he?"

Something in the way he said it made me smile like a loon. It was like when you see a small Chihuahua squaring up to a boxer. Plucky. I giggled.

"What's funny?"

"Nothing, just Sam really is a huge loser."

Wesley looked at me and cupped my chin and started to kiss me again. It was adorable. At first, I felt a little self-conscious. I hadn't quite worked out if I wanted Sam to see me kiss this little fella, but he was very charismatic and funny. When I came up for air, I noted that Sam had turned round to face the front of the bus, and he and Ellen were sitting in silence. I now felt a new warmth in my stomach. Smugness, I think.

"Lizzie, we're not really getting up for a picnic, are we?" I asked.

"Yes, Nat, we are."

"For fuck's sake," I muttered.

The next day Lizzie woke me up early and I was not happy about it. I hadn't taken 'date ready clothes' for Sunday. I was hungover and still making sense of the night before. Like all drunken nights, they tend to reappear in flashbacks. The worst ones coming into the mind slowly and with purpose. Each moment worse than the one before and being enveloped in embarrassment. I'd typically need a week to recall the whole night and sort the memories into those that were pure fun and those that needed to be locked away and not reviewed ever again. I was not going to get the space to consider the thoughts.

Reuben and Wes promptly turned up at Lizzie's at 11. *Sigh* I really had hoped not to see them both again so soon. Wesley was still short. Such a pity as he was really very handsome. By way of reference, he looked very much like Chris Martin (Coldplay fame) in their Yellow Video. However, no matter how funny, handsome and as good a kisser as he was, I could not get over his height. Being a tall girl with buxom proportions, I didn't need the added hurdle of dating a short bloke. I decided I'd just be cold and distant, and he'd lose interest. We drove to Haworth. One of my most favourite places on the planet. It's so pretty and picturesque. We wandered over the moors just chit-chatting nonsense. Wes told us that he was at College and studying A' Levels. He wanted to be a CAD CAM designer. I was actually kind of interested in this and so we ended up having a really good conversation. We were all then hungry and so walked into the village and chose one of the fish and chip cafes for lunch. Not quite a picnic but it would do. Overall it was a really pleasant date.

"So, when can I see you again?" Wes asked.

"Well, I'm travelling back to uni tomorrow and won't be back for several weeks," I said limply.

"So, shall I come over to stay with you then?" he asked.

Crikey – forward much?

Reuben started laughing.

"What's funny, Rubes?" Lizzie asked.

"Little Wes wants to get his leg-over and lose his V card," he joked.

Poor Wes looked mortified. OK, so this was disappointing news, and I reflected I was not some charity worker.

"I'm not offering a deflowering service, guys!" Lizzie shot me a look which mostly was the look you have when you see a new-born puppy.

"Fuck off, Rubes," Wes said. He was really not happy.

"Well, of course, you both can come, but it's not cheap on the train."

"Rubes can drive us, can't you, Rubes?"

"Well, I can but not for a couple of weeks as I've got stuff on. Family stuff," he added.

On the way back to Lizzie's, I gave Wes my house phone number and agreed he could call me and that night he did. He explained that he'd been online and found prices and times and could come over that weekend – if I wanted him to? So, I agreed. I'd meet him at the train station the following Friday night. I'm not so sure why, as I was still totally hung up about his height. He was arriving on the 7.12 pm train. I arrived at 7 pm. *Maybe he won't turn up? Perhaps he won't be as short as I remember?* I felt kind of sad thinking that he might stand me up though. I was surprised at myself for having those thoughts. Maybe I liked him more than I thought? I saw the arrivals board announce the train's arrival and my stomach flip-flopped. What would we say to each other? Would he think I was still 'fit' or now just 'fat'? I saw him in the distance with his rucksack on his back and holding a skateboard. *OK, cool points for sporting the skateboard,* I thought. As he walked through the exit gates, he saw me and smiled. A huge smile. I felt myself smile back, it was big and turned quickly into a grin. The ice was broken.

"Hey."

"Hiya, am I glad you're here! I didn't know what I was going to do if you didn't turn up," he said.

His vulnerability was sweet and made me affirm, yes I like you. We went to the bus station pub. It was the closest place where we could chat without having the awkwardness of being sat on a bus. I was also not ready to introduce him to my housemates just yet either. He updated me on how Rubes was. They'd discussed our picnic date, and Rubes had declared that he wasn't that into Lizzie and had only kept the date for Wes. I was slightly touched at this as in truth we had had a really good time. In fact, I hadn't noticed Rubes and Lizzie struggling to find things to talk about on the date. We exchanged details on how our respective weeks had trundled along and then the journey to Hull. It was now 9 pm, and Wes asked me how long it took to get to my house. This was the cue to get a bus to the house. When we got there, the house was dark and empty.

"It's massive," Wes said.

"Yeah, it really is."

I showed him around the shared parts and then led him to my room.

"Wow, this is huge," Wes gawped.

"Yup."

You could sense the tension in the air. We were standing in my bedroom. No one else in the house. My huge king-size bed was all nicely made.

"Are you hungry?"

"Starving."

"Well, just at the back of the house is a road that has a hundred takeaways to choose from, shall we go and get something to eat then?"

"Yeah, cool."

It was now entering into a strange part of the meetup. We'd genuinely been delighted to see each other, but we'd soon left it too long without any intimate activity. No kissing or holding hands etc. So this was the part of the date where my inner monologue was advising me:

'He doesn't like you like that now he's seen you again.'

'Yeah he's definitely gone off you.'

'He's probably trying to work out how he can get back home.'

'Yup, he's stuck here and hoping there's a spare room.'

Sometimes my inner voice is a fucking bitch! Sensing that I was in my head, Wes started to talk to me.

"I was dead worried that you wouldn't fancy me and ask me to go home," he chuckled nervously.

"Well, I haven't made up my mind if I fancy you or not," I winked at him and bit my lip.

With that, he grabbed my hand and pulled me into him and kissed me. Softly. It was amazing. My head went fuzzy, and butterflies circled in my stomach. When we came up for air, I was grinning.

"I think I've settled that then," Wes said and gave me a cheeky wink.

He put his hand into mine, and we walked hand in hand up the avenue.

We chose pizza and took it back to the house. Some of my housemates were now in and milling around. I introduced Wes to them, and they were nonplussed. From his

178

perspective, it must've appeared quite rude. There wasn't really any comradery amongst the tenants. We simply shared services and space. There were a couple of cliques in the house, and I wasn't in either. It didn't bother me most days. Some days it did as I had romanticised that I'd meet amazing people at uni and we'd end up living in some sorority type house and be thick as thieves. I quickly learned that student life really isn't like that. Most students lived in mixed accommodation, and all had some weirdo share their house. Maybe I was the weirdo in this house? Probably, but no matter. The rooms and facilities were too good to move out. It got to about 12 am and we were both yawning. Both a bit worried about the sleeping arrangements in truth.

"OK, I'm knackered so am going to turn in. You can either stay up and watch TV or come to bed with me," I spurted.

I was feeling very nervous about bedtime, but I was now so tired that the need for sleep was forcing me to be bold.

"Oh, I'm tired too, so I would rather just go to bed."

We went into my room. I stood behind my changing screen and got into my PJs.

"I'll use the bathroom first."

When I returned from the bathroom, Wes was in his boxers, socks and wearing his tee. He had his washbag and dutifully used the bathroom. I opted to leave the bedside lamp on his side, and facing the wall got into bed. I felt Wes get into bed and roll to face the opposite direction.

"Night," he said.

"Night."

He turned the lamp off. *I hate this. I can't sleep as I feel weird about how we just said goodnight. I now have feelings of awkwardness and ickiness. Harrumph. I now wish that I was braver so I could say something and be able to get some sleep.* Just as I was berating myself for being so bloody shy, I felt Wes roll over. I then felt him put his arm around me and move into me – *So we are spooning. There are those damn butterflies again!* While this felt lush, I knew that I was not getting any sleep anytime soon. I rolled over to face him. We were now looking at each other with small smiles. He then leaned in to kiss me. Softly and gently. There was now a real rush of blood to my lady parts. *FUCK! I really want him,* I thought. *I want him NOW!* So, I began to pick up the pressure and pace to signal to him that we were on! Green to go. His free hand went straight to my breasts, and he fondled, and it was good. Sensing his hesitation, I slipped my hand into his boxer shorts. I noted that there was a slight movement backwards on his part. I removed my hand from his shorts and stopped kissing him.

"We don't have to do anything but kiss if you don't want to, it's OK!"

"No, I want to – like, really want to. I just don't want to be crap."

"You won't be."

With that, he took my hand and moved it back to his boxer shorts.

In the morning, I awoke, and he had his arm wrapped around my waist. It had been a very good night. A very good night, indeed. However, right now, I needed to pee, and somehow get his arm off me without waking him. This, of course, was an impossibility. When I returned from the loo (of course, I'd brushed my teeth) Wes was stirring. He stretched and yawned. He then flung open the duvet and patted the bed. I liked this. As soon as I was in, he was on top of me. Kissing, caressing. He was ready to go. I was ready to go. So we went at it, after which we collapsed, smiling.

"What are you laughing at?"

"I'm not laughing, I'm smiling," I said.

"OK, what are you smiling at?" he asked.

"Erm, what do you think I'm smiling at?" I asked coyly.

"I hope you're not laughing at me?" he asked. I could see that vulnerability in him again, and it was a huge turn on.

"I'm smiling at you because you have just made me smile."

I looked very deeply into his eyes and leaned in to kiss him.

"Oh, that's OK then." He smiled back.

Pretty safe to say that most of the day was spent in that bed. Giggling, smiling, grunting and feeling satisfied. We did eventually have to get up and eat. Plus, Wes was super stoked about going to Spiders nightclub. I had told him all about the club and how cool it was. I'd even taken the night off so we could spend the time together. It's hard not to have a good time at spiders, and so inevitably Wes was blown away by it. The music, drinks, clientele, friendliness and me. Something for every sense. As we travelled back to mine in the taxi, Wes was chatting away merrily.

"My friend Gaz would love it here. The club is awesome."

"I'm glad Hull meets your expectations."

The next day it's the day to take Wes back to the train station. We'd learned a lot about each other during this weekend and mutually decided that we really liked one another.

"I'm gonna try and get Gaz to drive me over next Saturday, can he stay here?"

"Yeah, sure, but on the sofa, unless one of my housemates is away."

"He won't mind that. You'll really like him. He's a top guy."

"Yeah, OK. As long as it means I get to see you, that's all I care about."

During the next week, we called each other, and it was easy to tell that Wes was into me. He confirmed that Gaz was up for driving over and we agreed that they'd be in Hull after 7 pm. Wes and Gaz both worked Saturdays at the local Morrisons supermarket. They had to put a shift in and so would have to travel over after they'd finished. I'd managed to secure a room for Gaz as Lucy, one of my housemates who is super annoying, was going home for the weekend. I'd actually managed to switch the Friday shift for my Saturday shift, so I was free to host the pair too. I heard the car pull up and so as not to look too eager, I went to the back of the house to the loo. I'd let one of my housemates go to the door and meet them, and then I wouldn't look too eager. I could hear Peter at the door, talking to them. I nonchalantly meandered up the hallway corridor. I could see Wes's face, and he was searching behind Peter to see me. My heart was literally pounding with excitement and nerves in equal measures. I'd spent the last two hours quaffing my hair and perfecting my makeup. I'd spent the entire week trying on different outfits so that I looked just right. Of course, I didn't want to look like I'd been working too hard, though. It's a delicate balance to strike. His broad grin when he saw me made it all worthwhile. We were still at a very awkward stage of this fledgeling relationship. We'd only actually seen each other four times. Gaz was wondering what's happening during this exchange of goo-goo eyes.

"Nat, this is Gaz," Wes said while kind of shoving Gaz forward.

He was tall, skinny with a mop of curly brown hair. He was actually very handsome, and even though he was clearly feeling like a spare wheel, he smiled.

"Hey, Gaz. Shall I show you your room?"

"Yeah, please." And with that, we did the grand tour and arrived at Lucy's room.

After Gaz and Wes unpacked their things, they both had a quick wash. It was now nearly 9 pm, and we decided to go get some food. It turned out Gaz wasn't much of a talker, and he didn't appear to have an opinion on anything. We rocked up to a local Chinese restaurant and got a table.

"So, Gaz, are you at college too?"

"No, I'm in a gap year before I go to uni."

"Oh right, so which uni are you going to go to?"

"I haven't decided yet."

I wasn't really sure how to process this as if he didn't have a deferred place, then how did he intend on going anywhere. I then quickly concluded that I actually did not care. It was immaterial to Wes and me, and right now, my priority was re-establishing the 'haze' of being a newly loved-up couple. I was looking at Wes and if only he could read my mind which was screaming 'kiss me already'! I needed confirmation that he hadn't gone off me. Yes, he'd turned up but what if when he'd seen me again, he'd changed his mind? Thankfully, Gaz needed to visit the bathroom and so left us alone. I smiled sweetly at Wes. I couldn't think of anything to say, and I was pretty sure if I tried to speak, I'd have no voice. It had diminished in the swell of excitement coursing through me.

"I missed you, ya know," Wes said while looking at me.

He was not able to keep eye contact for the whole sentence and so his view trailed to the floor. I took this as a sign he's into me and equally worried that I may have gone off him.

"Me too," I managed while averting his gaze.

Wes then leaned in and kissed me on the lips. It was damn electric. My mind was fuzzy and I could feel it whirling. The same feeling you get when you are crossing the fresh to drunk line. Gaz returned and spoke,

"Oh don't be doing mushy couple stuff all night. I'll puke." And we all laughed.

We went to Spiders and got there about 11pm. The staff were all keen to speak with me and give me free cocktails and I was happy to oblige. Wes took Gaz off to show him around the club – like it's his local. I could tell that Gaz was impressed.

"Here, I got you a Pan Galactic gargle blaster." I passed him a pint glass.

He really wasn't too sure what was being given to him, but he quickly took it and took a drink.

"What is it?" he enquired.

"It's the most popular drink we serve. It's a pint of gin, vodka, tequila, crème-de-menthe and Galliano with Cider. It's delicious, and you'll love it."

He did. I thought it best to simply get one of every cocktail. As you can imagine, Gaz was arseholed quite quickly. He was lolloping about, and so we felt it best to take him back to the house. This in truth suited Wes and me, and it meant we had more of the night ahead of us, at my home and in my bed. We'd paced ourselves and were just the right side of giddy to have a very satisfactory night of sex. It wasn't mind-blowing, but it was exceptionally competent. In the morning, we could hear Gaz retching. *Poor lamb,* I thought and laughed. I laughed so hard I woke Wes.

"What's so funny?" he asked, rubbing his eyes.

"Listen, you can hear Gaz."

We both listened. We both laughed. Laughter turned into kissing and kissing turned into more. We'd used the three condoms in the pack the night previous and Wes hadn't got any more.

"Don't you have any?" he asked me.

"I might have, they gave us a load during freshers week, and I think I kept some."

I knew I damn well had a drawer-full (I'm a safety girl). So, I feigned a mini search and miraculously found one. It was blue and flavoured. Wes didn't need to know the latter. After we'd enjoyed the blue condom, Wes pulled out.

"Oh, oh shit!"

"What?"

"The condom's not on my knob?" he said with a visible expression of surprise and panic.

"It must be," I added.

I looked down and could see clearly it was not. It must have come off inside me – wait a minute, and with that, I began my own search expedition. I could see Wes was grimacing and I wasn't too chuffed about having to mount my own search and rescue mission. I felt about and seriously could not feel or find anything. Drawing a blank, we decided it must have somehow slid off and would be in the bedsheets.

So, we both got up and searched every millimetre of the bed. Nothing. OK, it was time to retrace our steps.

"Wes, you are going to have to have a look," and I pursed my lips.

I'm not happy about this but – I said to myself in my head, *I'm now considering that if it's in me and I don't get it out, I could get toxic shock or poisoning or something?*

"Whoa, I'm not doing that," he said and looked ashen.

"Wes, we have to find it. It can't just have gone missing!?" I responded.

He was now closing his eyes, grimacing.

"Look, you don't have to look, just have a feel around."

Reluctantly Wes complied. Nothing.

"What the actual fuck – it has to be here somewhere."

So I left Wes to go back over the bedding, and I decided to go to the toilet to see if having a wee might flush it out somehow. Of course, it didn't. To this day, I have no idea where that condom went? We got up, washed and dressed, and Gaz suggested they make a move. It was relatively early, but the mood had gone. Gaz was visibly grey, and Wes and I were now in a funny place. It was too young a relationship to have been fishing around my vagina for us to laugh about it. So we gave each other a nod and off they went. Wes rang me when he got home to let me know they'd had to pull over three times for Gaz to be ill. This, however, had not put him off and so Wes told me he'd asked if they could both come that weekend. During the week, Wes and I spoke each night. Gaz had been really impressed with the club and Hull and so had arranged an open day visit to the uni. As it happened, it was Friday of that week, and so they were going to come over Friday and go home Saturday night. They'd managed to swap their supermarket shifts for Sunday. When they arrived Friday, I was prepping for a lecture. It was a quick hello, and then I took them off to the University to drop them off at the meet and greet point. We agreed to meet back at my place for 6 pm.

"So how was the tour, Gaz?"

"It was excellent. They've got a really great science programme, and I think it would be a beneficial course," he added, sounding seriously positive about it.

"Do you have the right grades?" I enquired.

"Yes – it's 2 A's and 1B, which I already have."

"Oh yeah, I forgot you're on a gaaaaaap year," I mockingly added.

I suddenly saw Gaz in a new light. He was actually very attractive, tall, dark and handsome. He'd got 2A's and a B (better than my grades), and he had his own car. *Oh crap! I'm beginning to fancy Gaz*, I realised.

Wes began to distract me and clearly wanted to get me on my own. I was happy to oblige. I was going to be working tonight, and so Wes and Gaz were going to come to the club, and we'd leave together. Gaz was really excited about this as it meant he wasn't the third wheel. He and Wes could knock about together and have a 'lads night'. That was cool by me. I'd get to see all my workmates, earn my wage, not have a hangover the next day and still get great sex when I got home. I'd call that a win-win.

I was right. It was great sex. Wes had now had sex 8 times and was behaving like a pro. Whether he'd been getting advice from his friends or the internet, I did not know. His confidence, along with his moves, were getting better and more energetic. As we cuddled that early morning I caught a

187

glance of him looking at me. It struck me that he had developed genuine feels for me. I hadn't really thought that we would or were going to do that. I'd just assumed he'd understood that this was all a bit of a silly fling. A chance encounter that had escalated into a few great dates. As I drifted to sleep I began to think about the future. What if we actually had a future as a couple? I'd been fishing so hard and concentrating on catching a fish I'd only really worked on the attraction bit. I'd not considered the bit where you'd got a fish on a hook. What then?

Gaz and Wes got up first. I could hear them laughing with my housemates in the kitchen. I was always a bit nervous about this part as my housemates weren't my biggest fans. That week we'd had a considerable fall out as they'd asked me to contribute more to the electricity bill because apparently 'I used the washing machine' more than anyone else. Like WTAF! I used it once a week. Who wasn't using it once a week the scruffy, smelly bastards?! So the atmosphere had been a wee bit spikey. Then when I told them Wes and Gaz were coming over, there had been some comments about 'extra people in the house using the water and electricity for showers'. Looking back at this time, I still think I lived with a bunch of pricks.

I agreed with Wes that I'd go back home that weekend so he could attend his Saturday shift at Morrisons. Gaz was a bit peeved as he had really wanted to come back to Hull that weekend. Nonetheless I was kind of psyched that he'd insisted that I go to his and hang with his friends. I saw that as a positive step. He wanted to show me off to his crew. To announce he had a girlfriend. Initially, I had been severely panicked at this thought (I was still not happy about his age or height), but he'd won me over, the little scamp. I bought a train ticket (fancy) and set off home. I was going to my home in Silsden, which is where I would base myself. I'd then take the train back into Shipley to meet Wes. He said he'd call me at lunch from work, so I knew what time to set off. Until then I hung with my mum and dad and we caught up on student life and my studies. Of course, I told them everything was excellent, and I was doing fine, which was an utter lie. I had missed so many lectures and seminars and was falling way behind as I'd spent the last year pretty much applying myself to the pursuit of fishing. When I wasn't out with friends, I was planning nights out with friends. When I wasn't out or planning on being out, I was in bed napping. It was exhausting going out as regularly as I did, and having a late-night Friday, Saturday job and then an all-day Sunday job. I was pooped.

Just after 1 pm, the home phone went. I knew it was for me. As soon as I heard it, I became immediately excited. Another sign I was also catching feels for Wes.

"Hi."

"Hi, can I please speak to Nat?" an unfamiliar voice asked.

"Yes, this is she, I mean it is Nat," I spluttered.

"It's Matt, I'm Wes's mate from work. He's asked me to ask you if it's OK if he doesn't see you tonight as he wants to have a night on the PlayStation with his mates, but he's too chicken to tell you." I then heard lots of laughing in the background.

"Is Wes there?" I asked.

"Yeah, I'll put him on," the voice responded.

"Hey Nat," Wes said.

"Haha! Wes, very funny," I added in a droll voice.

"Err, the thing is, Nat, I did forget that I'd promised the lads at work that they could play a Fifa tournament 'round mine tonight. I can't let them down."

I could hear the tension in his voice.

"Oh, OK, that's cool. I don't mind hanging around yours with your mates," I added.

In truth I did, but I wanted to be the cool, chill, laid back girlfriend.

"Ah no, that's not what I meant. I meant I fancied a night with my mates only."

Now I'm not confident what other girls would have done at this point. Was I supposed to:

- Be chill and say 'yeah sure – I get it, babe.'
- Be annoyed but cute and get him to tell me how much he was going to miss me
- Bring the rain and call him out on his shit

Well, I'd have preferred any of those to what actually happened. I went into what can only be described as a whiney bitch mode. I'm ashamed to say I snivelled a little, asked him to reconsider, asked him why he'd prefer to spend time away from me and then begged him to see me. At that moment I just heard him say 'I'm completely over you – you ugly hoe'. Now, of course, he didn't say that – but that's what my mind heard.

"Look, Nat, I wasn't really looking for a girlfriend, and the thing is you live so far away," he muttered.

Oh my gosh! He is actually now dumping me.

"Why didn't you say this before I spent £50 on a train ticket, gave my shifts away at work and sat at home, you prick!" I yelled down the phone. I was livid now. My body filled with rage. My mind raced and several competing thoughts all attempted to connect to my conscious mind – but brain fog had now enveloped my brain. It felt like I wanted to claw my skin off or run, run hard and fast somewhere.

There was no way I was now staying in K-town – I needed to be back with my people in Hull. I didn't want to mope around at home in front of my parents and the injection of adrenaline that was coursing through me made it impossible to sit down or focus. If I set off now, changed my ticket, I could be back in Hull for Saturday night. So, I grabbed my bag and told my parents I was off. I caught the train from Silsden to Leeds and changed in Leeds to get back to Hull. I was transfixed with replaying the conversation. *He'd rather play on his games console than be with me!* I was fuming. By the time the train pulled out of Leeds I'd moved through anger and had landed straight back into self-pity. I noticed that there were now tears running down my cheeks. *What the fuck is happening? I didn't even like the virgin midget! Why do I care?* I thought. But I did. I seemed to have really caught the feels and they were now visibly rolling out of my eye sockets and drenching my cheeks. Onlookers couldn't work out if they should ask me if I was OK or simply leave me alone to cry. I crouched to hide my face – I just wanted to be alone. Half an hour into the journey, I was all out of tears. I literally had no more water left in my body to spare. I now just had the 'headache' that comes after you've sobbed for a long time. My nose was all stuffy, and I'm sure my makeup had run off my face. I must've looked a real state. I took the bus home and hoped no one would be in. I didn't want to have to answer my housemates' questions about where I'd been or why I was back early. When I got back to the house, I immediately rang my girlfriends to see who was free to go out that night. In succession, they all had their excuses; no money, boyfriends, assignments! When I'd called my last friend, I put the phone down and could feel the tears coming back up to my face. The phone rang. *Yes!* I thought. *It must be one of my friends deciding that they do want to go for a night out.*

"Hello, Nat speaking," I said feeling optimistic.

"Hey, Nat, it's Wes," a sullen voice said.

"Wes?"

"Yeah, I just wanted to see if you were OK and that you got home OK?"

I was super confused and annoyed right about now. How dare he follow up dumping me for his mates and games console with a sweet phone call.

"Yeah, I'm OK. I'm back in Hull," I said, suddenly feeling dumb as of course he knew I was back in Hull, he was calling me in my Hull home. Duh!

"Yeah, I rang your house, and your mum said you'd decided to go back to Hull."

His voice trailed off.

"Yeah, I thought I might as well come back and hang with my friends as I'd just been dumped," I added.

"Yeah, I'm sorry, Nat. I don't know why I said we needed to break up – I just wanted a night with my mates. I feel like I haven't seen them in ages."

There was a long pause.

"Well, you can see your mates whenever you want to now. You just needed to have told me, you don't have to be manacled to a girl you know."

I was saying this being quite pouty now. I wasn't really sure what was happening. Was he now ringing to say it'd been an enormous mistake and ask me to forgive him? A number of scenarios ran through my head but all the while I had nausea in my stomach. I'd cried a lot of tears. I didn't really want to allow Wes to make me cry ever again.

"Hey look, I think it's for the best," I started to say.

I was as surprised as him to hear this come out of my mouth.

"I mean the long-distance thing is tough, then there is the age thing, and finally, there's the experience thing." I knew the last comment would sting his fragile ego.

"Oh, right yeah, you're probably right," he mumbled.

"Well, take care, Wes, and most importantly, I hope your game evening lives up to all the hype."

With that, I put the phone down – triumphantly. I felt much better. I'd gone from being the dumped party to the dumper and strangely enough, taking back the control of the situation made a huge difference. My head was still thick, and I was still sniffly, but I felt 100% better.

The Car Journey from Hell

I decided to go back home and spend the weekend with my family. I could do with some distractions other than men, sex and uni work. Mum had had her 6 weeks of chemo now and so it was a waiting process next. At this time the university computers lab lead engineer had announced that they were launching the university's first ever intranet site. One of the features was to be a rideshare section. I felt it unlikely that anyone would be offering lifts to K-town but I was keen to investigate the service. It was open to both Humberside and Hull students. I logged on and checked out the lifts being offered and to my astonishment there was a lift being offered that Friday evening with a return Sunday night. They were asking for a contribution towards petrol money. I responded to the advert and they asked me to be ready by 7 pm on Friday and wait at the bus stop outside the university grounds. They'd be driving a white Fiat Panda. Excellent!

I arrived promptly with my weekend rucksack. I was a little nervous in case the driver was in fact a serial killer but also a little excited to see who was going to K-town. I could see the car and so walked over to it. I bent down to look through the passenger window and knock on the glass. My heart stopped for a moment. Our eyes locked. I think we were both in absolute disbelief. It was Harriet. Sam's Harriet. The love of his life, Harriet. Completely frozen and now aware that I was just staring at her, she leaned over and opened the passenger door.

"Hello, Natasha," she said.

"Hey."

"Are you going to get in?" she asked.

"Yeah, sure."

"I guess this is awkward for us both – huh? But we are both Sam's exes now so it doesn't have to be that weird," she added.

"I agree."

And with that we set off in total silence. That journey took two hours. Two intensely quiet hours. As we finally arrived into K-town, I spoke.

"Thanks for the lift. Here's my petrol contribution. I suggest I get the coach back."

"Probably best. I'm going to drop you off here as I'm going 'round to see Sam's new flat."

With that I got out of the car. My mind instantly wondering where Sam now lived. She'd dropped me at the bottom of Cavendish Street. This was one of the main roads that dissected K-town. It was actually my favourite. One side was truly bland and modern looking with a McDonalds and the other was a beautifully restored Victorian covered walkway. The Victorian side had a glass canopy that was held up by iron work columns. They were really ornate and pretty. They were painted black and gold. The shop fronts were semi modern with eye-catching display windows. The shops themselves never seemed to make it past a year of trading. We'd had toy shops, hairdressers, joke shops, electronics, beauty and schoolwear to name but a few. We seemed to have a particularly high number of health food and holistic shops but nothing stuck. No matter, the fact that the shops couldn't stay afloat didn't matter. It didn't detract from its charm and beauty. I crossed the road so I could walk up the canopied roof walkway. I liked to think about all those people who would have promenaded along this street. I'd imagine the ladies in their beautiful dresses, twirling their umbrellas and the handsome men promenading with them. At the top of the street was the town's library. A truly beautiful stone built building. I had spent a lot of time in that library as a child and had fond memories of the children's book section. I felt my mood lighten. I had shaken off the car ride and was looking forward to spending time with my folks.

Getting Help

When I got back from K-town, I realised how distanced I had become from my family. I didn't recognise them or their lives. I'd been so engrossed in my own burdens and follies that I had failed to even look up. I'd become very proficient at living in my own head. On the coach ride back from K-town I allowed myself to think about the previous months and the memories made me feel deeply sad. I also for the first time gave myself permission to acknowledge the fact I'd been thinking about suicide, daily. Some days it was at the front of my mind and some days it was just reoccurring thought like – oh, I must remember to have a drink soon.

There had been one particular evening where I had gone to bed (I don't recall this) and when I awoke there were empty bottles of paracetamol and vodka bottles wrapped in my bed sheets. When I awoke I was genuinely puzzled. I don't drink Vodka – ever. Why was there an empty bottle of Vodka wrapped in my bed sheet? I then saw the empty bottles of paracetamol. 2 bottles with a count of 30 tablets. I don't recall buying them. Nor do I understand how they were also on my bed. My mind tried to reason why there were empty paracetamol bottles and an empty Vodka bottle. Why would I have chosen to neck paracetamols with Vodka? It plagued me that day but my consciousness had stricken it from my memory. I ran a couple of alternative scenarios through my mind – like maybe a housemate had left them on my bed to encourage me to take my life? Each scenario I thought of seemed as ridiculous as the notion that I had actually attempted to kill myself. I simply deleted the thought as it was far too puzzling to unravel and so it must be a false memory?

I decided on that coach journey to get help, to go see my doctor. Dr Nayar had been my designated doctor since I went to Hull. She was a really lovely doctor and very welcoming. The morning of my appointment I was scared. What if I told her I'd been thinking about suicide and she rang my parents? What if she sectioned me? I'd never get a job if an employer knew that I'd been sectioned.

"What can I do for you today, Natasha?" she asked.

I didn't know if I'd find the courage to speak. I had been rehearsing some form of words in my mind for days and was hopeful they'd make it out of my mouth.

"I seem to be having a hard time coping with life at the moment, and find I'm thinking about suicide a lot." I dared not look at her.

"Have you made any firm plans on this?" she quizzed.

"No, not really. I just can't seem to stop thinking about it. I just feel sad and depressed all of the time."

I had decided to definitely not mention the paracetamol and vodka incident – as I didn't know what I'd actually say.

"OK, Natasha. I think we should refer you to the psychologist to have a longer conversation. They can explore your thoughts with you and see what further help we can offer. You will receive a referral letter and an appointment will come to you in the next 2 weeks."

I wasn't sure how I felt about this. Firstly, two weeks is a very long time and secondly if I now had a record that included a referral to a shrink then that was a sign of certainty that I was not normal. In fact, I was 'mental'. The appointment rolled 'round and with trepidation I attended. It was a female psychologist and I wasn't with her for long. She asked me about what may be upsetting me. I recounted that my mum had cancer, that I didn't get on with my housemates, that school was harder than I thought it would be and I was failing and that I'd recently been dumped. She asked me about my periods and I commented that I did suffer with PMS. She said she'd write to my GP with her advice.

I received a phone call at home. It was Dr Nayar. She explained that the psychologist had said that I was having 'normal' responses to life's stresses and strains and that I should continue to take evening primrose oil. She said she'd leave a revised prescription for me and wanted me to take 6 capsules a day. So that made it official – I was, in fact, normal. Looking back at this time makes me both angry and sad. PMDD wasn't understood back then and so many women were diagnosed with PMS. Evening primrose oil had no proven effects on PMS yet it was the number one treatment. It subsequently got pulled from the NICE guidance. Finally, the diagnosis conversation was less than 40 minutes, before which the psychologist had collected enough information to meet a neat and tidy outcome. I have learned that when presenting to clinicians they are often quick to take first impressions. If you are not presenting as dishevelled and maniacal then you are not deemed to be in any immediate risk. Furthermore, if you present with clarity and are succinct and appear to be highly functioning, this too leads to misdiagnosis. I'm living proof that you could have attempted to kill yourself on Monday morning but have it all together (from the outside world's perspective) by Monday afternoon and receive a clinical prognosis of 'normal'. The diagnosis doesn't help. In fact, it creates even more mental torment for me. Is this it? Is this what a normal life feels like? Can I, or do I even want to live my life in this way?

The Friendzone

During the final semester, I met a guy outside of Silhouettes nightclub. He was very tall, 6' 4", willowy, with a shaved head and a milky complexion with beautiful brown eyes. He had the smoothest, poreless skin which was luminescent. He wore blue jeans, Etnies trainers, some sort of graphic tee and an anorak. A cool anorak and wore a Vans backpack. The night I met him he looked really forlorn. I could make out his face which was illuminated by the streetlamp outside of the club. I'm always drawn to people with sadness behind their eyes, it's like a powerful magnet. I walked over towards him and smiled squarely at him. He smiled back.

"Hey," I said.

"Hi," he said back with a southern accent.

"I've not seen you here before, are you new to Hull?"

He guffawed at me. "Ha! No, I've been here 4 years. I'm in my final year."

"Oh, right. Perhaps I mean, is this your first time at Sils?"

"Oh right, no I've been before, but normally I'm here with my girlfriend. Well, ex-girlfriend."

With that, he pointed. I followed his finger and saw a girl with white, bleached blonde hair. She was mega cool.

Perfectly styled in every way. Hair, makeup, outfit. The trifecta.

"Oh," I squeaked.

"Yeah, it's a bit awkward as she dumped me this week for the guy she's brought with her tonight. It's the first time I've seen him." I could sense the heartbreak.

"Did you go out for a long time?" I asked. I'm not really sure why I asked this. I felt obliged to follow up.

"3 years."

"Wow that is a long time then. That must suck?" I added.

He gave me a look that I'll never forget. It was as if I'd reached into his heart and just held the pain for a moment so he could have a moment of relief. He smiled the warmest smile.

"I'm Justin."

"I'm Nat."

We chatted for a little while and then my friends called me for the obligatory walk home. I saw Justin weekly after that at Sils. We'd always gravitate towards each other. I introduced him to my circle of friends and we kind of adopted him. Being with a girlfriend for 3 years fucks up your friend circle. You tend to not have one. With every passing week, I grew to know him a little more. He was reading Classics, formerly lived in Reading and didn't have a clue what he was going to do after uni. Join the club! Even though we spent a lot of time together, I never once tried to get off with him. I just had a feeling that he was out of my league. He was courteous, friendly and warm and so I just assumed he wouldn't be interested in me. A couple of times, I thought I caught him looking at me in a way that may suggest he was interested in me; however, I'd manage to talk myself out of that conclusion and would then feel even more ridiculous. I felt that logically he had sensed my friendliness and in truth, lack of boundaries and gravitated towards me as his rescue package. I'd saved him from being friendless and lonely and thrown him a lifeline. He was grateful, and that is why on the odd occasion I'd find him looking at me with those beautiful eyes. I had entertained the idea that he'd formed some sort of attachment to me and I with him – but the notion it could be romantic on his part just couldn't be so. There is no way that a handsome, intelligent, sensitive and funny guy would be interested in me. Nope, I'd concluded he was definitely out of my league, and I would have to just practice acceptance of this fact. My friend Sonja (from the Wednesday night crew) eventually asked me one night,

"So are you and Justin together or can you fix me up with him?"

I didn't care too much for Sonja. She was a short girl, with multi-coloured hair and a labret piercing. She seemed cool enough but in truth, I think I was jealous of her. She was everything I wasn't. Petite, cool, aloof and had many facial piercings. I wanted to appear nonchalant and said:

"No, Justin and I are just hanging out. If you want, I'll try and set you two up?"

"Yeah, that'd be cool."

So I spoke with Justin. He seemed uncomfortable initially.

"She's too cool to be interested in me."

So I gushed with platitudes,

"Don't be daft. You're a great looking guy who is cool in his own right. You're funny, sweet and a total catch."

I felt sick saying these words. I meant them, but I wanted to not be telling him in this way. So with my exceptional sales skills, I got them together. I was gutted. They went out on a date. Sonja fed back it was 'OK' but that he was 'really shy and boring'. This really pissed me off. *He's not dull, FFS. He is shy. You just need to stick with it, and then he'll loosen up,* I thought. A couple of weeks later, they came to Sils together. I was heartbroken, but my face was a different story. I noted Sonja was off with her two best friends and Justin stood like a lost sheep. I wanted to go and talk to him so badly, but I couldn't. I was hurting so much. I look back at this and realise it was probably one of my biggest regrets.

Anyway, the following week they had split up. I was so relieved. We were only weeks away from the end of term and finals were approaching, so I had to ditch Sils for a few weeks. I thought about Justin daily. I now had 6 weeks until my first Final. I'd had news that mum was in remission and I felt elated. This was the best news ever. I felt uplifted and energised. I was going to smash my finals and I was going to get a 2:1. I organised my revision timetable and let everyone know I would be on lockdown until after the exams. I applied my brilliant mind, summoned every ounce of will and I poured myself into study. I read all the chapters in my work books, made colour co-ordinated notes and tested myself heavily. If you were watching this period of time in a film it'd be a montage – like the one where Rocky gets ready and fit for his fight. Turns out this is the effect of hyper-focus and standard Adhd behaviour. The ability to squeeze in 1 years' worth of study in 6 weeks and ace my finals.

One day, while revising there was a knock on my bedroom door.

"Yes," I shouted.

The door opened, and to my absolute amazement, it was Justin. I didn't know how he knew where I lived. My head was racing, I hadn't washed my hair, I had on basic makeup, and I had on a shitty outfit. I was revising after all.

"Surprise," he said.

"Woah! What are you doing here?"

I was genuinely in shock. I was laid on my stomach on my bed. He towered over my bed. He looked so very handsome, I could feel the butterflies in my stomach. They were going crazy, and I was trying hard not to grin like a bloody fool.

"I brought you some revision food," he said. With that, he pulled out a bag of Satsuma's from his rucksack and a 4 pack of mars bars.

"You need vitamin C to make sure you don't get ill and then sugar to stay awake."

I giggled.

"That is so thoughtful of you, Justin. That is so cool of you. Thank you."

He, too, was smiling and looking bashful.

"Hey look, I've finished with finals, and so I'm going back home tomorrow."

I was struggling to follow him and understand what he was saying. My auto-response was to numb my feelings so he couldn't sense how I felt about him.

"Oh, wow. That'll be well weird. You're going back to live at home with your parents?" I asked.

"Yes, and yes. It'll be an adjustment for sure," he gave me a no lips smile.

"So I thought I'd say goodbye and give you my address as it would be nice to stay in touch."

He proffered me a piece of paper. I could see there was tiny join up writing upon it.

"Yeah, that's a good idea. I'll defo send you a note to let you know the outcome of my degree for sure."

"Well, best of luck Nat, not that you'll need it."

I jumped up, and we hugged. It was swift and surreal. I can replay the visual, but I can't bring the feeling back. I had been so busy numbing myself to not let slip how I felt that I'd been unable to process the hug. Regret number 2.

With that, Justin said he'd better go as he still had to pack his stuff up and awkwardly left.

I was in emotional hell. I felt elated that he'd thought enough about our friendship that he'd stopped by. He'd thought about his excuse and purchased fruit and chocolate. He'd prepped his address. Surely this all meant he liked me too? Then the crashing thoughts that he was leaving. The very next day. I had no way of contacting him in Hull. To reach out and tell him how I felt. Finally, the inner bitch who reminded me that there was no way he 'liked me' as he was out of my league. I can tell you not much revision took place for the next few days.

I decided to write to him. Why not? He'd given me his address so yes, I'd write to him. I wrote a perfectly acceptable, platonic letter asking him how he was. Had he found a career yet? How was it being back at home and he wrote me an entirely platonic letter back. I didn't write again. I knew I would never have the courage to tell him how I felt and to keep up the platonic relationship meant mostly hurting myself with every letter. Regret number 3.

Things Always
Come to an End

I'd taken a real battering over the last 18 months. Emotionally and spiritually. I'd searched out comfort in all the wrong places. I'd attempted to self-soothe my aching heart by seeking out distraction, and when that hadn't worked, I sought out ways to self-sabotage my life, friendships and university. As I cram revised for my finals, I found that I was able to create space. I'd always been able to apply myself. I think the fear of letting down and disappointing my parents was all the fuel needed. The more I concentrated on my studies, the clearer I found my thinking. I was able to process some of the encounters and began to see I'd created a very unhealthy relationship with myself. I wasn't able to handle everything – as let's face it, there was a lot to process. I found myself thinking about Justin. Why had I assumed he was too good for me? This particularly bothered me. I spent days revising and the evenings reflecting. I distanced myself from my friends and just kept my head down. At the end of the exams, I was exhausted. Mentally, physically, emotionally and spiritually. I stayed in bed over the following week to recuperate. I missed a lot of calls from friends, and I was OK with that. The fogginess that I had been experiencing over the last 18 months seemed to be lifting. I'd describe it as feeling like I'd had an elastic band tied around my brain – just constantly squeezing my mind. Just enough that I could never quite get clarity but not enough that others would notice.

I seemed to be on the mend. I knew that moving back to K-town would be a disaster for me and so persuaded my parents to let me stay in Hull. They'd agreed that until my results were published in July, I could stay, but if I hadn't found a job by then I was to go 'home'. So with my new-found clarity, I began to search for a job. My neighbour Andy had suggested I apply for some of the graduate intake schemes. Great idea! Well, except all had passed their deadlines except 2. That was OK – I'd apply to them both. I was contacted and offered an interview for one of them. *Brilliant,* I thought. It was to be a 3-day assessment centre in Rugby. I'd told Page, and she'd suggested we go out to celebrate with Silhouettes. It felt wrong to go to Sils knowing that Justin wouldn't be there, but life must go on – I thought. So with my university career over and new horizons ahead, we had a night out at Sils. It was to be a night that changed my life forever.

Remember the guy with the long ginger curls at the eclipse nightclub? Well, I finally met him that night. We've been together for 23 years and married for 21. He's way out of my league, but I decided not to let that stop me this time. I also got the placement on the graduate scheme. 32,000 applications and 18 were selected. That's not the end of my story, of course. I have struggled on and off for the last 30 years but finally, in 2019, I was diagnosed with Emotional Unstable Personality Disorder. The diagnosis was a relief. Just like anyone with BPD I've thrown myself into research upon receiving the diagnosis. I've come to understand it more clearly, and in doing so, it's helped me accept, forgive and laugh at some of my actions, thinking and decisions. I'd already started writing this book 12 months in advance of my diagnosis. So looking back at this with a new lens, I can see all the trademarks of Emotional Unstable Personality Disorder.

Emotional Unstable Personality Disorder

Someone on a Facebook Emotional Unstable Personality Disorder group shared these words and I think it sums up BPD really well:

When you are Emotionally Unstable
Sadness feels like suicide
Anger feels like murder
Distance feels like abandonment
Joy feels weird and unknown
Being in love feels like you are not worthy and you are an inconvenience
Happiness is an unbearable euphoria
Losing someone feels like dying
Feeling normal feels like emptiness
Now imagine all those feelings in one day.

It's not my place to pontificate about EUPD, PMDD or ADHD as there are lots of resources that can be accessed, but if you have any inkling you have some of the same symptoms I showed then you should definitely get help. Book an appointment with your family doctor – don't put it off. 1 in 4 people will experience ill mental health every year in the UK (and that number is achieved by looking at those who go to their doctors). Imagine if everyone who had an issue went to their GP. I think we'd be looking at 1 in 2 having mental health issues. That is why I conclude my story that I am, in fact, normal. I have 3 diagnosed mental health conditions, PMDD, EUPD and ADHD. I also have asthma, suffer from vertigo and migraines. I'm also a successful wife and mother – author now. I'm a loyal friend and thoughtful daughter. I take medicine daily for both my mental and physical ailments.

I haven't started treatment yet as there's a long waiting list in the UK. So I have spent many months now seeking out information, joining support groups and reading books on treatments. I am pleased to learn that there are a number of really cool upsides of EUPD and ADHD to keep a balanced view, I'm sharing the positives that manifest with these disorders.

You Have Deep Empathy

Many people with EUPD identify as being an 'empath'. An empath is someone with so much empathy that they feel others' pain as their own; they sometimes cannot separate their own emotions from others'. Certain psychological theories may explain why this is. It might be due to overactive activity of your mirror neurons, unique wiring of your brain, specific hormones in your physiology, or a volatile childhood environment in which you were 'trained' to become hyper-vigilant. You might have to detect early warning signs of your parents' anger to protect yourself and your siblings. Because of your personal experience, you know what it means to be in emotional pain. When others are sad, anxious or grieving, you offer an unspoken understanding. Psychologically, others can feel soothed by your presence. Spiritually, those who suffer know you speak their language.

You Are Deeply Perceptive

Research has found people with BPD can read facial expressions and subtle shifts in moods more accurately than those without BPD. Many people with BPD and their friends even joke they have 'psychic abilities'. This perceptiveness comes with its blessings and perils. It may make life more difficult as you see hypocrisy, injustice and deception everywhere. People might feel threatened by you as they did not want to be seen through. It may take you a while to find a way to use your intuition without offending others. Once you have, however, the ability to be perceptive and intuitive is a powerful skill that brings you much personal and career success.

You Can Channel Pain into Art

Many people with EUPD channel their pain visually, poetically, musically or otherwise. Historically, gifted and talented artists, writers and actors/actresses have made meaning out of their mental distress and existential anxiety. The pain of EUPD can be so massive that it is beyond words. This is when the arts become its channel of expression. By doing so, you refuse to be a victim. By expressing your soul via creative means, you are reaching out to the world. Somewhere, someone is waiting to know there is someone out there feeling what they are feeling. Once you have found a language for your emotion, you are on your way to inspire the world.

You Have a Deep Capacity to Love

Another myth about BPD is that people with the condition cannot love in the same way everyone else does. This is demonstrably false. Whether or not they show it on the surface, people with EUPD love and care with their whole being. The push-pull pattern and instability they have are a result of your trauma. Having been wounded deeply by abandonment, rejection or neglect early in your lives, intimacy becomes a challenge. It is not that you don't want to love, but your fears and insecurities hold you back from being the best self you can be. You love fiercely and can be hurt deeply, so it can be challenging for you – especially at the start – to relax in a relationship. When you feel safe enough, however, you make a sensitive, passionate and extraordinary friend, parent and life partner.

You Know What It Means to Have an Invisible Illness

Unlike a physical injury or disability, EUPD is invisible. It is, nevertheless, one of the most painful conditions anyone could have. You might also have suffered from other invisible trauma such as childhood neglect or emotional abuse. People often dismiss the suffering of someone who looks fine on the surface. But you know what can lie beneath the surface of a facade. Your story also offers you a deep well of compassion. At your best, you are liable to champion the voices for others.

Many people with EUPD are gifted activists who champion for the rights and voices of others.

You See the Beauty in the World

Being a naturally sensitive person, you are pained by the collective pain of our world; but on the flip side, you also have a profound understanding of beauty. You don't take love for granted, 'little things' such as a single line in a song or a gesture from a romantic partner can be almost overwhelming. You feel the world with a different vibration, and you are vividly alive. You know despair, but you also know deep love and ecstasy. Being able to feel so keenly is a downside when the emotions are challenging, but it is also a gift.

You May Not Feel It, but You Are Exceptionally Resilient

EUPD does not break you; it shapes you, forces you to look inward, and make you a stronger human. Like a tree, you bend, but you do not get destroyed. You have been through so much pain and despair that you know every day is a gift. The longer you have to learn to live with EUPD, the more resilient it makes you. You become a warrior. You withstand not only the symptoms but also the natural knocks that we receive as we go through life. Having been through EUPD and coming out the other end, you are stronger than you think you are. At your core, you are not your mood swings. Beyond the surface, the fluctuation is a core self that is determined to be alive.

ADHD and EUPD have very similar symptoms and so one can be diagnosed over the other. It was only in 2021 that I was diagnosed with ADHD too. I'm still learning about this diagnosis but what I have learned so far is making a lot of sense to me.

The Hidden Chapter

When I was in my twenties, we used to go to HMV and spend hours looking through the racks of CDs. I'd always imagined finding my one true love there. They'd be looking at the Pearl Jam section, and we'd meet. We'd realise we had a love of the same music and he'd ask me to go for a coffee. Well, statistically, I spent more of my time at university during my degree in the local HMV than I did in the library and not once did any man speak to me in the Pearl Jam section. I'm talking about hundreds of hours, people! What I did get from investing that time were some remarkable records. I particularly felt my time was well served when you'd stumble across a hidden track. So to those of you who have got this far – enjoy this hidden track.

So I went back to my hometown. I was collecting all my belongings as I was making a move to the Midlands to start the graduate scheme. My friends Sarah and Lizzie insisted I have one last night out at The Grinning Rat. Farewell drinks. Of course, I was happy to oblige. Life seemed to be working out for a change. I'd found a place to live, I'd scored a very well paid graduate place on a national graduate scheme, and I'd found a man. A man who was handsome, intelligent, kind, and thoughtful and always scores 10/10 every single time we kiss.

I agreed to meet Lizzie and Sarah at 8.30 pm. They both still had Saturday jobs and would meet me after they finished. I felt like a visitor now in K-town. Strangely it didn't feel like home anymore. I was looking at it through a new lens. It seemed kind of run down and the people walking past me seemed to be trudging. I felt kind of sorry for these poor souls, destined to spend their lives in this insignificant town. I, on the other hand, was about to start an exciting new life in a major city, pulsating with life, pace, purpose and opportunity. I went into the pub and noticed that nothing had changed. The chairs and tables were all in the same place. The windows were dark with road soot and not much light spilled through them, making you feel like you'd entered into a cave. I went to the bar and ordered my usual – a pint of sweet cider and blackcurrant. The place was stark, and so I could choose any table I wanted. I decided to sit near the jukebox and felt like it's serendipitous that on my last night I would get to choose the music. So I spent some time looking at the possibilities. I decided that I would pay £1 and pick 5 songs.

1. There she goes – The LAs
2. This Charming Man – The Smiths
3. Friday I'm in love – The Cure
4. Resurrection – The Stone Roses
5. There she goes – The LAs

Luke and I met through the love of The LAs. He had worn a gig tee, and I had spotted it. I'd been at Keighley's other premier nightspots – Champers. That was a real rough townie

216

nightclub. At chucking out time, a massive brawl had started, and the police were arresting folk left, right and centre. As I was only 17, I was sure I'd get arrested, and my mum and dad would learn that I wasn't around at Rachel's having a sleepover but was drunk at a notoriously awful nightclub. I had spotted Luke and his tee and made a beeline to him. I hooked my arm onto his and said,

"I know you don't know me, but I love The LAs and so tell me where you saw them."

Thankfully he'd been too surprised to do anything other than answer my question. That night we had spent 20 minutes discussing the LAs and having our arms hooked to each other. It was during this encounter I fell for him. Of course, you know the rest. Six months of my life spent trying to get him to make a move. Followed by one awkward telephone conversation and a date that never happened.

Listening to 'There She Goes' always made me feel sad, but it was kind of a happy-sad. The feelings were a blend of the thrill of the night I met Luke, the joy and laughter of the six months of our friendship tinged with the pain of being stood up. I still loved that song. As I sat at my table for one listening, I saw the door open. Expecting it to be Lizzie and Sarah, I was poised to jump up and say hello. It wasn't the girls though, in a very surreal turn of events, it was Luke. I hadn't seen him for eight months. I was not expecting to see him ever again. We were now the only two people in the whole of the pub (except the barman). He smiled. My stomach had butterflies, a swarm of them. I instinctively smiled.

"They're playing our song," he said as he walked toward me.

"Well, they aren't – I am."

"How's you?"

"I'm really good, thanks. How are you doing?"

"Yeah, I'm good. I'm a fully qualified architect now. Got my own business up and running."

"That is so cool, congratulations. I too now have a job. Finally finished uni. I'm here about to have farewell drinks with the girls."

His face flushed with sadness.

"You can't be sad about that; you should be relieved it means there will be no chance of you running into me again," I said sarcastically but laughing to let him know I was teasing.

As usual, Luke looked at the floor, and I thought I could see he was blushing.

"Hey, why don't I get you a drink? Gin and tonic if I remember correctly?"

He nodded, and so I got him a drink. I was feeling quietly confident about myself, and I had a good deal to feel optimistic about. I now had a job, an exciting future, real friends and a cracking chap and so I felt like I wanted to put this relationship to bed.

"Luke, can I ask you a question?"

"You are going to ask me why I stood you up, aren't you."

"Yes, why did you stand me up?"

My heart was racing. I'd finally learn why after all that effort and all that time we spent together, he chose to stand me up. I felt a lump in my throat. Maybe I didn't want to hear the answer. I could feel the brain fog begin to fill my head.

"I didn't. I didn't stand you up. I got to the Rat Trap at midnight and I came upstairs. I saw you stood in the corner. You looked so beautiful. You had on a green blazer and white shirt. I saw your friend Sarah was nearby and panicked. I ran back downstairs to get control of my nerves, you were just too pretty, cool and popular to want to go out with me. So I bottled it and got a taxi home."

He was talking to the table. Too scared to make eye contact. There was a quiet pause. He looked at the table and me looking at him. The words are now ringing around my ears. He hadn't stood me up. He had just been too chicken to come over to me. In his mind, I was out of his league. My little brain was awash with excitement. He had liked me! He had fancied me! He'd just been shyer than me. This was possibly the best news I'd ever received. My stomach was now flooded with excitement. I was positively euphoric.

"Well, you dope!" I said mocking him.

"I was crushed that night, I really was. I'd spent ages getting ready for you." I was laughing now.

I popped my arm around his shoulder and squeezed him. "It wasn't meant to be, huh?"

Luke turned his head to look at me, and for the first time, I felt like he'd found his courage.

"I did like you, Nat. I was just never confident enough to tell you."

We continued to talk about life, our separate plans and the ease by which we had always spoken was back. Luke's friend Kevin joined us.

"Did he tell you he turned up to your date but chickened out? If I hear one more time how beautiful you looked in your green jacket, I'll retch," he said.

We all laughed but the adage that Luke told his friends about it, told them he thought I was beautiful was terrific to hear. I was grinning like an idiot for the rest of the night. Luke and Kevin moved on, and we said goodbye. We knew it was our final goodbye.

I think of Luke a lot. Twenty years later, I bumped into his friend Kevin back in K-town. He gave me Luke's phone number, and I texted him. We now exchange a couple of texts a year. I'll tell him about a band I think he should check out and he'll let me know about a gig he's been to. I'll always feel something for him.

Lightning Source UK Ltd.
Milton Keynes UK
UKHW020815201222
414194UK00019BA/211